The BOOK of EVERYDAY RESISTANCE

Edited by
Lori Perkins

For more information contact:
Riverdale Avenue Books
5676 Riverdale Avenue
Riverdale, NY 10471.

www.riverdaleavebooks.com
Design by www.formatting4U.com
Cover by Scott Carpenter

Digital ISBN: 9781626017054

Trade Paperback ISBN: 9781626017061

First Edition, March 2025, Second Edition June 2025
Riverdale Avenue Books would like to thank you for reading this copy of *The Book of Everyday Resistance* by gifting you one free book from each imprint, which you can download at the link provided:

www.preview.mailerlite.io/preview/1098983/sites/136486432257607665/0kJ9TD

Resist much, obey little.
—Walt Whitman

It is from the numberless diverse acts of courage and belief that human history is shaped. Each time a man stands up for an ideal or acts to improve the lot of others or strikes out against injustice, he sends forth a tiny ripple of hope, and crossing each other from a million different centers of energy and daring, those ripples build a current that can sweep down the mightiest walls of oppression and resistance.
—Robert Kennedy

"When fascism comes to America, it will be wrapped in the flag and carrying a cross."
—Sinclair Lewis

"We can either have democracy in this country or we can have great wealth concentrated in the hands of a few, but we cannot have both."
—Justice Louis D. Brandeis

Acknowledgments

Putting together a book like this is a team effort. In addition to eternal gratefulness to the wonderful contributors who graciously gave me their work free of charge, I am eternally thankful to the incredible people who work with me:

Camilla Saly, who read through everything on a moment's notice, and then wrote an essay about the collapse of Hungary when I asked her to;

David Valentin, my Assistant Publisher, who always has my back, the wind beneath my wings;

Scott Carpenter, our creative and intrepid Art Director, who takes my wacky ideas and makes actual art out of them:

And **Judi Fennell,** our book designer, who knows what I need before I even do and works tirelessly around my crazy deadlines.

Table of Contents

Introduction:
Resist, Repeat, Resist

On election day, my world changed, like most of yours. I was thrown into a pretty dark depression, and I wondered what the future would hold not only for me, but for my city and my country.

I grew up in Washington Heights in New York City in the 60s and 70s, a neighborhood known as the largest concentration of German Jewish Holocaust survivors in America. Many of my friends' parents had concentration camp tattoos burned on their arms, and I heard their first-hand stories of escape and survival. When the German Jewish population in Washington Heights thinned it was replaced by an immigrant population of people from the Dominican Republic who came here after the fall of Trujillo's dictatorship. From them I heard stories about the Disappeared: the resisters who were taken away who never returned. So the effect of living under fascism was not a fairy tale to me. I saw what it did to people I knew and loved.

Growing up I often asked myself what I would have done if I had been an adult-ish person or lived in Europe during World War II. I imagined myself as brave, so I thought I would resist to my fullest extent, but now, as an adult, I realize how dangerous it can be, and how much is at stake. As an adult with a home and a business in a time where our every move and thought can be traced, I asked myself if I could hide people in my New York City co-op like the Miep Geis family did with Anne Frank's family, and sadly concluded that I am not that brave.

I knew I couldn't get passports to people fleeing the country like Raol Wallenberg had done during WWII.

All my money is tied up in this small independent publishing company.

And then I realized that that was my resistance.

My very small staff and I put this book together in six weeks, while

1

editing all the other books already scheduled for publication. I had no idea what the book would look like or who would submit. I have been stunned by the power of these essays, both individually and as a whole, by ordinary people, as well as people who should have been too busy or famous to even acknowledge my request for their thoughts in this fraught time we are living in.

The last essay that came in is the first essay in this book, *This is Why* by Christopher Golden, who was one of the very first writers I ever worked with at the start of my career as a literary agent in the 1980's. I read on Facebook that he was attending protests and I asked him if he wanted to share his experience. Between Tesla protests, he sent me his essay, and it made me cry, even after reading and editing all the other amazing pieces in this book.

It really made me aware of just how saddened I am by what is happening in my country.

But I am also so heartened by the essays in this book.

Putting this book together made me really understand that there is no one way to resist. We all resist every day in every way.

And we need to keep doing it in every way every day.

To that end, I am hoping to do multiple editions of this book until it truly is The BIG Book of Everyday Resistance I want it to be.

Riverdale Avenue Books is offering the book for free on all digital platforms, so please share it with everyone you feel will benefit.

Resist.

Repeat.

Resist!

—Lori Perkins, Publisher
March, 2025
lori@riverdaleavebooks.com

THIS IS WHY
A Message to People Like Me
By Christopher Golden

I was born in 1967. Growing up in the 70's and 80's, I had the enormous good fortune to live in an America that still believed its own myths. My family had its struggles, but I look back on those days now with a strange sort of guilt. Despite the litany of ugly things that could be said about the era of my youth, in comparison to 2025 America, it was a wonderful, innocent time. Of course, society then was structured to keep it that way for straight, white, cisgender boys like me. The Civil Rights movement had changed the nation (to a certain degree). The Vietnam War was over. The 70's were all about "Have a Nice Day" and smiley faces. The Catholic church of my youth was one of folk music and inclusion. I grew up believing that the moral arc of the universe really did bend toward justice, and that my country would continue to evolve toward true equality for all people.

For a long time, I believed we were moving in that direction. It's true that for every two steps forward we took a step backward, but laws were made, one after another, to help level the playing field, and to protect people who were not made in the image of what the worst of humanity perceives as the "factory default." Marriage equality became the law of the land. American society seemed to embrace the truth, that sexuality was not a choice. Our culture embraced the truth that diversity is healthy and desirable, that each of us deserves to share in the freedom promised by our founders: life, liberty, and the pursuit of happiness. There were factions who pushed back, hatred still simmered, but I believed we were on the road to fulfilling the only aspirations that truly matter as a nation. Growing up, I never would have imagined how many trans people I would know, and call my friends. When I imagined how tortured they must have been by confining themselves inside identities that could only feel like costumes, or prisons, I was elated to see them embrace their true selves, and show them to the world. This was a

3

promise that we were on the way to being the America I'd always believed we would one day become. The kind of society I was always taught—both in church and in school—that we all believed in.

I was such a fool.

The first election of Barack Obama to the Oval Office was the pinnacle of my faith in the future of the United States of America. It's been all downhill from there. Generations of spoiled white boys who'd been told they were special—that they were better and more important than anyone who wasn't white, straight, or male—raged with bitterness and resentment. Their parents and grandparents raised them to feel entitled to power, and to believe that any deprivation in their lives was because the things to which they were entitled had been stolen by "others." Society had been carefully constructed to continue the illusion that they were better and more deserving, and any effort to shatter that illusion they could only see as an attack on the societal position they saw as rightfully theirs.

Now, here we are. Petulant, raging white men accumulated unima-gineable wealth, manipulated ignorant, also raging white men without a pot to piss in, so they believe that the reason they are not as wealthy as their idols is because of women, or Black people, or immigrants, or LGBTQ+ people. Rich or poor, these hideous men are full of spite and resentment and cruelty, and they want to hurt anyone whose existence ever made them feel like maybe they weren't as special as mommy and daddy promised.

They are desperately trying to put the genie back into the bottle. They'll go to any lengths to make that happen. If they have to jail people, they will happily do that. If they have to hurt people—and, let's be honest, even if they have to kill people—they will rejoice in the pain and sorrow that ensue.

It's no surprise that the people who are their immediate targets are out there protesting, are speaking out online and in public spaces, are gathering, are committing acts of civil disobedience. LGBTQ+ folks, BIPOC people, immigrants, women, Native Americans… they raise their voices to say there is no putting the genie back into the bottle. Our society is diverse. These putrid fascists can't erase that fact. The fantasy these men have about living inside an episode of *Mad Men* is just that, a fantasy. But standing up to that fantasy is going to be difficult and painful and costly in so many ways.

I could avoid all of that. If you're a straight, white, cisgender man like me, you could avoid it, too. You could stay silent and turn away. If you do that, you'll still suffer the economic hardships that will come, but maybe

4

you won't be targeted. You'll still have to live in the oppressive fascist state these men envision, but they won't single you out. You could keep your head down and your tongue silent.

But then you'd be a Nazi, too.

I want the nation I was taught we were building toward. I want each of us to be treated with dignity and allowed the rights the founders promised—life, liberty, and the pursuit of happiness. I want equality and justice. If I were to stay silent when others are being attacked and oppressed, when the bastards are trying to shove the genie back into the bottle, I'd be just as bad as they are. Hell, I'd be worse.

There are no superheroes. Nobody is coming to save us, to build the nation we're meant to be striving for. There's just us. Me, and you. The fascist oligarchy is depending on you to let it happen. They're doing everything they can to make you feel like there's nothing you can do, but they're lying to you. The most important thing for you to do is be vocal, and be seen. Oppose them loudly and publicly. When there's a gathering in protest, get out there.

I attended a protest a few days ago with a dear friend. In a sea of more colorful faces, with more colorful clothing and colorful flags, with much more experience at these things and greater comfort with the usual chants, I'm sure we looked quite unexciting. We are, after all, that mythical "factory default." But we were far from alone. There were plenty of others like us who aren't among the fascists' immediate targets, and it lifted my heart to see. It's vital that the cameras recording these events show the true diversity of those who stand against cruelty and tyranny. But they only way to do that is for you to be there. Show others that you won't be silent, in hopes that you will inspire them to also raise their voices, to open their eyes, to come out and protest.

Simply put, either you believe in equality and justice for all, or you don't believe in equality and justice. If you do, then stand up. Speak out. Fight for love and kindness and empathy, and against hatred and cruelty and greed.

Silence truly is complicity.

Christopher Golden is the *New York Times* bestselling author of such novels as *Road of Bones, All Hallows, The Night Birds,* and *The House of Last Resort*. With Mike Mignola, he is the co-creator of the *Outerverse* comic book universe, including such series as *Baltimore* and *Joe Golem:*

Occult Detective. He has also written for film, television, video games, and animation, and he co-wrote and co-directed the Audible original series *Slayers: A Buffyverse Story*. He was born and raised in Massachusetts. Golden has been nominated for the Bram Stoker Award 11 times in eight different categories, and has won twice. He has also won the Shirley Jackson Award and the Audie Award, and his work has been nominated for the British Fantasy Award and the Eisner Award, among others. Golden lives in Massachusetts.

Swinging at Monsters:
Small Things Can Pack a Punch
By Michele Hornish

"Trick or treat!"

I couldn't have been more than five years old.

Dressed in a homemade bunny costume, the poofy tail sagged and swayed as I walked the neighborhood with my mother and sister.

Together with a neighbor and her son Drew, we had circled the block (which was a lot for me at that age) and came back around to the beginning. To finish off the night we'd trick-or-treat at the neighbors' house across the street, and then head home for the candy inspection (Gen Xers know what I'm talking about) and long-awaited sugar rush.

My candy bag was comically full and getting difficult to carry without dragging on the ground. It was such a good haul that the little strings dug into my still-chubby hands, but I wasn't going to complain about the weight.

The three of us kids approached the neighbors' front door, rang the bell, and waited. To one side of their front porch was a particularly menacing Halloween prop. At least seven feet tall and grotesque, it was uncomfortable to walk past.

But candy is candy, and sugar fosters courage.

Soon enough, the neighbors opened the door and smiled at our costumes, filling up our candy sacks. We dug around in our bags to see what we'd gotten, while we tumbled down the front steps.

It was as we walked down the driveway that I heard it. Or felt it. Or just sensed it in the way that little children sense danger.

Something was coming.

I turned to see that the grotesque, menacing Halloween prop had roused itself from the front porch.

Clip-clop. It lurched toward us in strange, herky-jerky movements that made it even scarier. *Clip-clop.*

I was paralyzed. Terrified. *Certain that this was the end.*

In times of extreme danger, we default to our factory setting. And that's when mine kicked in.

While Drew hid behind his mother's skirt, I whipped around to face the approaching monster head-on. It was now staggering down the driveway toward us, closer and closer. *Clip-clop, clip-clop.*

Terrified but determined, my little five year old hands grasped my candy sack for dear life…

And started to swing.

Around and around and around I swung that candy sack, building up momentum as I walked toward the danger that I firmly believed would be my demise.

The monster stopped… and leaned backwards, arms outstretched. *"No, no, no…"* I could hear it stammer.

It could speak?

No matter. **No mercy.** Nobody was going to take out my family.

If I was going down, I would go down swinging.

I gritted my teeth and let that candy sack fly—and knocked that monster clean off his feet.

And that's when I saw that the monster was really the tall neighbor boy we had nicknamed Big Bob, dressed in a scary costume, wearing makeup and a wig, and strapped into a pair of stilts.

I had knocked him clear off of those stilts and into the yard, where he lay, sprawled out, shocked.

Most of the rest of that interaction is blurry. But I do remember watching him scuttle away into the dark—fear in his eyes—as a bloodthirsty five-year-old Michele ran after him, bunny ears flopping, cotton tail bouncing, and candy bag swinging.

I had defeated a monster.

Lately it feels like we're surrounded by monsters.

The people and policies of the Trump administration appear before us as hulking, grotesque creatures. They're intentionally menacing, demanding that you see them as scary, intimidating, inevitable.

They seem to thrive on fear and see it as sport. But fear—and the paralysis that often comes with it—is also a key piece of their strategy. Their Gish gallop of bad policy is intended to scare you. To stun you into submission. To get you to hide behind your mom's skirt, rather than stand your ground and fight back with all the feistiness you can muster.

8

They want—perhaps even need—you to think that resistance is futile.

Because while they've got significant institutional power, they're not *all*-powerful. In many ways they rely on the compliance of the rest of us. They're like neighbor kids on stilts who thrive on terrifying those who are less powerful, but whose power depends upon the fear of the terrorized.

And the second that we (metaphorically) knock them off their feet, the spell is broken.

Whether you want to call it throwing sand in the gears or swinging the candy sack, the concept is the same.

Your compliance greases their wheels.

Your refusal—your defiance—slows them down.

Maybe you register your defiance with calls to Congress. Maybe with a letter to the editor. Maybe by organizing a precinct, registering voters, or recruiting candidates. Maybe by marching, or making art, or writing a blog, or organizing a lobby day in your state legislature…

There are many ways to get in the way. The point is to try. To swing, even if you may miss.

We may not be able to stop everything, but we can at least slow the descent. We can force them to expend political capital and burn time and resources fighting back against a whole horde of people who will not go quietly into that good night. That's time and resources they cannot expend somewhere else. Remember that by slowing their roll, we limit their damage.

So it's up to us to get in the way.

A side note that I've seen quite a few folks asking: where are the Democrats? Where's the coordinated response? Where's the leadership?

I hear that. I feel that. We need to see a lot more fire on our side, and trust me—I'll be pushing for it because we need to give them the steel backbones they need to stand strong for all of us. But I also know that we don't need to wait for a leader. *We've already got ways to fight back— right here, right now.* We call, we gather, we speak up—we get in the way in all the ways the grassroots community has gotten in the way for eight years now. We've got muscle and expertise—now coupled with the creativity and the passion of those who are new to this fight.

And one last thing.

My whole life I've been proud of that Halloween story, because I

9

knew even as a young child that the fight itself is noble, even if the outcome appears inevitable.

I feel the same way about today.

Fighting for humanity, decency, and democracy is *always* a noble fight—no matter the forecast, and no matter the outcome.

Friend, we have been given the gift of absolute moral clarity, coupled with the ability to do something about it. That is an opportunity. I hope you grab it with both hands.

Don't forget your candy sack.

Let's get to work.

Michele Hornish is a Red state Democrat, recovering lawyer, and the Executive Director of Every State Blue. She helps Democrats fight everywhere, one "small deed" at a time.

Want to Fight Back Against American Fascism? Know the Truth, Tell the Truth and Shame the Devil

By Amy Alexander

As I write this in early June, 2025, the 47th United States President is expanding his campaign to turn American small-d democracy into an authoritarian hellscape.

What can we do to resist?

One effective way to resist rising authoritarianism is to make sure that you are armed with the accurate facts of U.S. history: Whether your form of resistance is participating in street actions against armed and masked U.S. Immigration and Customs Enforcement (ICE) officers snatching up people from courtrooms and work-places, or writing legal briefs to counter discriminatory housing, education and housing policies flooding from the Administration's federal agencies, or boycotting retailers who capitulate to the anti-democratic Administration of President Donald Trump, the most important tool in your arsenal is accurate historical facts.

By reviewing the accurate facts of American history, you'll gain important data (human stories and statistical evidence) proving that a version of fascism has always existed in the United States. More than that, while its contours, shapes, expressions and applications have morphed over the generations, the result has been consistent: The preservation of an economic and social structure—a caste system—that keeps white men and women at the top.

If your vehicle and tactic of resistance, whatever shape it takes, is not informed by that documented, fundamental fact—and by the fact that White Supremacy animates and drives the 47th President of the United States—you'll fail to build the multi-racial coalition required to ultimately (hopefully) defeat America's WannaBe Fascists in the next presidential election.

Sadly, for example, I note that as armed ICE officers and U.S. National Guard service members posted up in Los Angeles in early June

2025 on orders of the corrupt 47th U.S. president who claimed that "gangs of illegal" Latino immigrants were "rioting" in the city, few Black residents turned out in the streets in solidarity with fellow Latino LA residents.

Why? In part, because millions of Black residents in California feel betrayed by Latinos who voted for the Republican who became the 47th president—choosing instead a gross, angry white man over the 2024 Democratic presidential nominee, Kamala Harris, a Black and Asian-Indian former California Senator and former Vice President who is also a native of Berkeley, California. Obviously, California's population of nearly 40 million people is not wholly representative of demographic and intra-ethnic dynamics in the other 49 American states—however, it absolutely *is* a microcosm of many key economic and political factors that play out nationwide, including the fracturing of former multi-ethnic voting blocs that solidly supported Democratic candidates since at least the mid-20th Century.

More than 30 years after legal scholar Kimberlé Crenshaw first coined the phrase "intersectionality," the structural, institutional pillars of her landmark critical race theory came into sharp focus for millions of Americans between 2020-2025. By the time the coronavirus had begun to sweep across the nation in spring of 2020, I was acutely sensitive to the ways that Crenshaw's 1989 critical race theory concepts are made concrete in America's institutions.

And while I did not envision an emergency scenario as dire and all-encompassing as the rolling crises of coronavirus pandemic, and by nationwide civil unrest in protest of systemic police brutality that occurred in 2020, followed by the re-election in 2024 of a corrupt, racist, failed businessman to the presidency, it had occurred to me many years ago that the array of structural inequalities in America, were not sustainable.

My form of resistance—finding, verifying, and sharing factual information about history and current affairs—is how I fight back.

In 2016, after nearly 25 years spent researching and writing about Black people and cultural politics, education, mental healthcare, and other central pillars, my "Aha moment" came when I first walked into the United States Department of Commerce building to start a year-long job as speechwriter and communication strategist to several Obama Administration political appointees leading an economic development bureau.

For many years leading up to that morning, my reporting on Black socioeconomic and cultural political topics as a professional journalist covered aspects of Crenshaw's seminal theory, which holds that Black women's ethnicity and gender exist intertwined with major legal, policy, and economic impacts on their life trajectory. Over the duration of 2016, though, as I immersed myself in the reams of U.S. Commerce Department contemporary and historic data-sets covering domestic and global economies and populations, a connection emerged between the personal framework of intersectionality, and the institutional manifestation of inequalities faced by Black women and other historically-under-represented populations in the United States. Where professor Crenshaw's theory of intersectionality stopped at women's doorsteps, the large infrastructure of it is so embedded across the American landscape that it hides in plain sight.

Why, for example, isn't it widely reported in U.S. news outlets that Black and Latinx women are the fastest-growing segment of small-business owners in America? Where are policy movements to close the big gap in access to capital that exists between growing numbers of Black and Latinx technology entrepreneurs and their white counterparts? Why are so few leaders of private sector organizations investing in solutions to healthcare disparities that negatively impact Black and Latinx populations? How many billions of dollars annually does America lose due to White-led systems that hoard opportunities and access, preventing ethnic minorities, older workers, and women from flourishing in business sectors?

I wrote talking points, speeches, and media advisories for a half-dozen economic development political appointees and experts at the U.S. Commerce Department economic development bureau where I worked throughout 2016, all focused on an Obama Administration White House initiative aimed at fostering growth of minority-owned businesses in Science, Technology, Engineering, and Math (STEM)-related business sectors. In developing these materials and interviewing economics experts at Commerce and in industry, I got an up-close look at population data housed at the U.S. Census Bureau, Economic Development Administration, National Institute of Standards and Technology, the National Weather Service/NOAA, and within all twelve of the innovation and business-related agencies housed at Commerce. I regularly cross-tabulated the history of economic growth in major American business sectors against regional, age, and gender groups to develop comparison metrics.

By January 2017, when Trump— a former reality TV show host and long-time real estate developer who had made his first serious foray into politics by running for president as the Republican candidate—was sworn in as America's 45th president, I had a clear understanding of how deeply embedded inequalities are within the foundations of the nation's major pillars. The interconnected nature of laws, policies, and financing in America literally have physical manifestation in the big buildings adjacent the White House—Commerce, the U.S. Treasury Department, and the U.S. Capitol.

For the first time, notwithstanding having written about Black people for more than two decades in America, I firmly grasped the full scope and size of systemic factors, including policies, legislation, and global and domestic economics, that kept America's inequitable systems humming along.

And by June 2020, as the nation reeled from thousands of coronavirus deaths, and hundreds of activists and regular citizens arrived in Lafayette Square near the White House and in other "town squares" nationwide to protest police brutality and Trump Administration anti-immigration policies and more, I experienced a mix of optimism and dread. Could the emerging multi-ethnic coalitions in cities across America significantly move these structural pillars, the very foundational moorings of the nation's justice, education, economic, and political and cultural systems to radical transformation?

Can the United States finally reorder its systems and hierarchies into an egalitarian framework following massive disruption caused by a lethal global pandemic, national and international civil unrest sparked by police brutality and the unprecedented racist words and policies of the 45th and 47th president? Can white and Latino voters in sufficient numbers learn, acknowledge and admit what is at the root of America's rising fascism—White Supremacy?

Since the early 1990s, through the journalistic tools of storytelling and the process of data-gathering and factual verification, I've been investigating and reporting on America's battle with itself over its original sin: the enslavement of Black people, and the decimation of Indigenous people at the hands of White people over centuries. The language, "All men are created equal" within the U.S. Declaration of Independence has been disputed, rightly so, by generations of women and men throughout the 20th Century. The monumental disruption of 2020, though, brought fresh anger to Black and other historically under-represented communities who said they are not willing any longer to countenance incremental changes—or to downplay the distress they experienced from the inter-locked pillars of inequality.

The stubborn historic through-line demarking the source of American inequality is clear: The seemingly intractable presence of white male supremacy across nearly all social and institutional pillars undergirding Americans' public and private experiences.

In my family, the elders always forgave us for our mistakes—as long as we learned from missteps and claimed responsibility. "Tell the truth, and shame the devil," my maternal grandmother, an Iowan who married a railroad foreman, would tell us. My people didn't hold the same expectation for White people.

Still, as a cautious optimist, I do believe in the innate promise of the human spirit, and in the value of calling a thing what it is, "speaking truth to power," as some activists put it. The metaphoric devil—and the White power structure that has denied Black humanity for hundreds of years in America—has been impervious to the truth. Yet I believe in the potential for all Americans in this 2025 fraught moment, to make significant progress toward achieving a "more perfect union"—even after more than two hundred years of the nation being caught in a cycle of intermittent legal, social, and economic gains for Black, Indigenous, and other historically marginalized people followed by White racist backlash.

So it is that I share this recommendation for resistance now: Your social media feed won't save you.

Your ability to gather and verify accurate information, and to marshal mutual-aid coalitions by coalescing around a commitment to defeat White Supremacy once and for all, is what is needed if America is going to defeat the current fascist movement.

Amy Alexander is a native San Franciscan and an award-winning Journalist, nonfiction book Author, and Strategic Communicator. Her interests are polymathic, with a focus on continual learning. In her collaborations with nonprofit, corporate, media, academic, and government organizations and leaders, she draws from more than 20 years of experience in producing news and information for mass audiences. Her work, which involves researching, writing, and producing real stories and messages, is aimed at identifying and promoting egalitarian principles, and actions.

The Lessons of History
By Camilla Saly

I am the child of Hungarian immigrants. In 1945, my mother escaped from Hungary. She experienced the Nazi occupation of Budapest, and was there while the Germans and the Russians were fighting in the streets for control of the city.

My mother, a Hungarian Jew, was saved from being taken to Auschwitz by Raol Wallenberg, a Swedish diplomat who saved thousands of Hungarian Jews by giving them diplomatic protection and clustering them into safe houses.

At the end of World War II, in 1945, the Russians entered Budapest. They called their entry "liberation," because they fought back the Nazis. But the Russian idea of "liberation" was occupation.

When Russian soldiers came to the house where my mother was hiding she had to strategize how to prevent them from raping her. First she made sure there was no liquor that they would find. Then, when they broke into the house, she immediately acted cordially, and asked them, in broken Russian, to see pictures of their children. Once they took out the pictures from their wallets, they were no longer interested in raping, she said.

There is a Hungarian "joke" about the Russian occupation that is not very funny. It goes that the only Russian phrase the Hungarians learned when the soldiers occupied Budapest was "davay chasy," which loosely translates as "Give us your watches." Yes, they were raping and pillaging.

As history reminds us, at the end of World War II the Russians occupied Hungary, East Germany, Poland, Romania, Bulgaria and Albania. In addition, as we know, the Soviet Union had occupied Ukraine, Belarus, Moldova, Lithuania, Latvia, Estonia, Georgia, Armenia, Azerbaijan, Kazakhstan, Uzbekistan, Kyrgyzstan, Tajikistan, and Turkmenistan. Today, some of these countries still struggle to remain independent despite Russia's efforts to occupy and control them.

Today you can still see large holes in some of Budapest's buildings that date back to the siege of Budapest when the two occupying forces —the Nazis (Germans) and the Soviets (Russians)—fought in the streets in 1945.

In 1956, the Hungarian people organized a revolt against the Russian occupiers and their puppet government. For 12 days during this Hungarian Revolution—between October 23, 1956 and November 4, 1956—brave Hungarian citizens tried to throw off Soviet control of their country, before the Russian tanks rolled in and violently subdued the uprising. The Soviets reoccupied the country, and it remained under Soviet control for another 35 years. Bullet holes from that conflict are still visible on otherwise elegant Budapest houses.

During the Revolution, there was a brief time of chaos when many Hungarians fled the country as the Russian tanks were rolling in. Among the thousands of Hungarians who fled at that time were my grandparents and my mother's cousins, who hid in a truck under sacks of potatoes for a perilous journey across the Hungarian border into unoccupied Europe.

My family has experienced the oppression and witnessed genocide of a fascist regime: the fascist Nazis, of course, but also the euphemistically named "Communist" regime of Russia, which was essentially fascist in its control and domination of its citizens and the citizens of the countries it chose to occupy.

In 1956 the United States chose not to defend Hungary. After World War II they settled for a division of Europe: Soviet control on one side and "Western Europe"—the countries that had been liberated by the United States military and embraced democracy—on the other.

Since the end of World War II, the United States has supported freedom and democracy in Europe, and provided security assistance and protection to prevent Russian expansion.

Now Trump is undoing that. He admires and seeks to support the fascist tendencies and occupational desires of Russia and Vladimir Putin—which have evidently changed little since 1945 in intent to occupy and dominate other countries.

The tools of fascism are: control of the populace by propaganda; erasure of laws that protect people equally; the infiltration and domination of the press; destruction of all opposition, art, and free speech; normalization of threats of violence; propagation of actual violence; destruction of the rule of law; control of the military and, ultimately, the imposition of "ethnic cleansing" directed at various groups—he Nazis chose Jews, gay people, Romany people, and opposition leaders, the Russians chose intellectuals, artists, journalists and political opponents).

Does any of this sound familiar? As someone who grew up hearing these stories firsthand, I can tell you that we are poised at the brink of fascism. Make no mistake. So let's not forget the lessons of the past. It's time to stop Trump and his fascist agenda now, before it is too late.

Camilla Saly is a lifelong New Yorker. She worked in the music business in the 1970s and then taught "at risk" youth in New York's Alternative High Schools for 26 years. She serves on the Board of Trustees of the Morris-Jumel Mansion in New York City and the Blue Hill Historical Society in Blue Hill, Maine. She is a co-founder PunkArchiveNYC, an archive dedicated to preserving punk and New York rock ephemera. Her essays have been published in *#Me Too: Essays About How and Why This Happened*, *Fifty Writers on 50 Shades of Grey*, and *Miss Pamela's Writing School for Electric Ladies*. She is a free-lance editor for Riverdale Avenue Books, as well as other publishers. She lives in Harlem, NY, where she is a writer, editor, musician, educator and activist for historic preservation.

Resistance as Survival
By Marc W. Polite

The confines of electoral politics in the United States has re-delivered what was rejected five years ago. This time, what Malcolm X described in a famous speech from the 1960's as "the ghastly alternative" has prevailed. Many are demoralized and terrified of what is to come. From an objective vantage point this is understandable, but it is counterproductive to remain in that state of mind.

Considering that a second Trump term will do all it can to harm the most vulnerable, resistance to it becomes necessary. We resist because looking at the history of Black people in the United States, we really have no choice but to resist if we are to survive. Whether facing benign neglect or open hostility, the struggle persists.

One way we can resist is to ridicule the idiocy. With an anti-vaxxer as the head of the Department of Health, there will be countless opportunities to sharply rebuke these people. It is necessary for writers to speak out against anti-scientific ideas. With wildfires raging, it will be vital to point out how wrong and dangerous these ideas are for the Environmental Protection Agency, the Department of Energy or the Fish and Wildlife Service. Do not give in to the ignorance that will be propagated, and expect no help from the establishment.

The announcement that Meta, the company that owns Facebook, Instagram and Threads, will now remove fact checking from these sites reminds us how disruptive the propagation of conspiracy theories and misinformation has played a role in undercutting public health concerns during the last five years. We can use this action by Meta as an opportunity to point out how untrustworthy these corporate-owned networks are for keeping us connected to one another. And that we should not rely on social media for our news and world outlook in the first place.

The resistance is not just narrowly against the incoming Trump

Administration, but against oligarchy in general. Whether it comes in the form of "tech bros" or climate denialists, pushing back on greed and grift is part of the task. Trump has already walked back on a talking point during his campaign, stating that it will be "hard to lower grocery prices." It will not be difficult to point out other false promises as events unfold.

I'm resisting by advocating for the rights of working people. I'm active in my union, and act as a conduit for information that will empower people. It will involve working locally on the state level to protect the most vulnerable.

I resist because of an awareness that the onslaught against "woke-ism" and antipathy for Diversity, Equity, and Inclusion (DEI) is just repackaged White Nationalism. There is a well of history that can be drawn from, which is one of the reasons why teaching it is being attacked.

This is a precarious moment, but this is where we are now. Leadership means pointing the way forward, and not always telling people what they want to hear. Those of us who are conscious and conscientious have unenviable tasks ahead of us. Encourage the disillusioned, and be akin to a lighthouse, helping people navigate through this moment of darkness.

Marc W. Polite is a poet and essayist. Born and raised in Harlem, New York, he writes about social concerns, labor issues, film, technology, and literature. His reviews and striking commentary appear in *The Amsterdam News, Poets & Writers, Black Star News, Madame Noire, The Grio, Time Magazine, The Atlanta Post, New England Informer,* and Harlem's own *Harlem News Group* and *Harlem World Magazine.* He is also a member of the Harlem Writers Guild, the oldest, continuously operating African-American writers guild in the world.

On Resisting Fascism of the Mind
By C. E. Monaghan

In the wake of the past few months with the naked specter of American Neofascism now openly descending upon our country, the topic of Capital-R Resistance has become a prevalent matter of discussion. To be clear, I believe that this is ultimately net-positive. However, I also firmly believe that attempts at Resistance are self-defeating if we do not first resist the reactionary thought-patterns that inform our worldviews. Fascism did not grow in a vacuum, after all, and the uncomfortable truth is that every single one of us is susceptible to becoming a Collaborator if we do not actively decide to fight it. We need to honestly contend with the reactionary worldview we all have stewed in for the entirety of our lives, both on and off the Internet. This is not a call to be kind or even polite to fascists. This is a call to extricate ourselves from the fascism within ourselves. If we cannot win the revolution within our own minds, we will not win the revolution outside our door.

First, I want to bring up a particular subset of self-titled "Internet Activists" who believe they are engaging in acts of resistance by directing mean-spirited slurs, homophobic punchlines, and transmisogyny towards Donald Trump, Elon Musk, and other poster-children of the MAGA movement. Let us call it for what it is: this is bigotry, and would rightly be condemned if directed at a marginalized person who isn't deemed "bad." In fact, this feeds into a fallacious mindset of the neoliberal worldview: *it's okay when we do it to them because we're the Good Guys and they're the Bad Guys.* This is how a fascist thinks and operates, and how they can easily convince the uncommitted, but gullible Moderate to perform their atrocities. We cannot allow ourselves to fall for this kind of thinking. Bigotry is bigotry, regardless of whom you direct it at. Furthermore, marginalized communities rightly recognize this behavior for what it is—a demonstration that we view the very people we claim to be allies with as either useful or expendable. This is how we plant the seeds for another resurgence of fascism within yet another generation.

Second, we must seriously contend with our own reactionary thought-patterns with militant mindfulness. One of the most universal ways that we engage in reactionary thinking is through the Just World Fallacy. To simplify the concept, this fallacy can be described as the idea that "good things happen to good people and bad things happen to bad people." In the abstract, this idea seems harmless enough, but in application, it leads to behaviors like victim-blaming or moralizing the success of influential people (Most notably, the inverse of this is, "Oh, this person turned out to be bad? Well, their work was always sub-par anyhow.") This attitude, when left unchecked, can take on dangerous forms that have us moralizing physical appearance, success, wealth, talent, and so many other factors that are the shadow of fascism's "cultural purity" versus "degeneracy" rhetoric that draws lines around communities and assigns values to them for the purposes of stratifying and enforcing a fundamentally eugenic hierarchy.

Third, we need to realize how often we engage in the self-defeating behavior of dealing in absolutes. Black-and-White, All-or-Nothing thinking is a prison for our minds, and it's one that fascism deliberately cultivates. One of the fundamental ideas of fascism is that *the existence of people deemed "inferior" to the chosen "superior race/class/gender/etc." is in and of itself an act of violence that must be reciprocated via mass violence against the inferior peoples.* The most famous example of this idea is the "Great Replacement" conspiracy theory that talking heads like Tucker Carlson have pushed, but goes back all the way to the Social Darwinists and eugenicists of the 19th and 20th Centuries. There is no room allowed for co-existence—only victory or total annihilation. You can see how the all-or-nothing mentality feeds into fascistic thinking, and how, left to its own devices, becomes the bedrock of atrocity. This too, we must strive to purge from our individual and collective consciousnesses alike.

Fourth, we need to look outside ourselves and actively engage in acts of love, compassion, and community. This does not mean you should be nice to your local fascists—after all, if you have a table of ten people and a fascist sits down and nothing is done about it, you now have eleven fascists at a table. That being said, we need to be forming community with those around us. Our society has pulled its mask off, and we see it for the cruel monster it truly is. And when societies turn cruel, an act of love becomes an act of revolution. From George Orwell's *Nineteen*

Eighty-Four to Suzanne Collins' *Hunger Games* series, acts of love, kinship, and community are rightly seen as existential threats to ruling oligarchs. We must hold onto the simple truth that love is stronger than hate—so strong and enduring that it lives on beyond even a singular lifetime. It is because we keep love alive that it can do so; we must not let that flame die within our hearts, lest we find out too late that we cannot light it again.

Finally, we must know, believe, and act like there will be an Afterwards. Even if we individually do not live to see an America finally free of fascism, that day will eventually come. Giving in to self-destructive, nihilistic thinking ("Nothing we do matters, so why bother?") is a strong temptation, but we only condemn ourselves to oblivion in the process. The fact is that we decide what matters. What has been decided can be un-decided. What has been done can be undone. Fascists can rob us of everything else—even our lives and dignity in death—but they cannot rob us of our ability to choose what matters and forge that into a dream. And because of that, fascism will never truly win, unless we allow it to kill our capacity to dream.

C. E. Monaghan was born and raised in the geographically and anthropologically diverse state of Arizona. Her firsthand experiences with disability, homelessness, and her personal journey grappling with her faith and her gender identity have helped shape her ideas—both artistically and politically. Perhaps unsurprisingly, her favorite author is Ursula K. Le Guin. When not focused on real-world politics and putting together her thoughts on writing from an artistic perspective, she is often trying to introduce her friends to her personal music collection, playing mad scientist in her kitchen, or reading and writing speculative fiction.

How This Boomer Resists
By Yolaine M. Stout

Perhaps because I was the only girl and the oldest, after four brothers, I grew up to be a leader, a rebel, a fiercely independent fighter for good things I care about. I fought despite the odds, the critics, and the defeatists. The resistance only made me fight harder. Win or lose, I gotta fight for what I believe in. It's in my DNA.

Besides my family, there is nothing more important to me than our democracy and our environment. In high school, I became fascinated by Hitler. While my family was out enjoying the beach, I was in our trailer absorbed in Shirer's *The Rise and Fall of the Third Reich* and *The Diary of Anne Frank*. I also read *Mein Kampf* because my history teacher told me not to. I needed to understand how such a holocaust of cruelty and war could happen. How could people just let this happen? Were there resisters? What happened to them?

Then, at age 19, I fell in love with an Austrian and moved to his country. Naively, I didn't consider what his father did in the war. The blood drained from my head when I discovered that my new father-in-law had been a Nazi officer. Oh. Shit! I sat back and considered how I would deal with that. I felt compelled to do what I had done in high school: study him. Study it. Learn to speak German fluently. Dig deeper. I lived in Austria for 12 years before finally getting a divorce.

Coming back to California, I became interested in cults after one of them tried to recruit me. (That was fun.) I studied cult strategies, their brainwashing techniques and how people could be vulnerable to them. Study those things long enough and you see very clear patterns. I saw many parallels to 1930's Germany and fascist techniques in general. You can predict their next moves.

After my soulmate of 30 years and my parents had just died, along comes a wealthy businessman named Donald J. Trump. He wants to run for President. I study him, and there they are—the patterns: the messianic ego, the black and white thinking, the obsession for control and attention, the authoritarian father figure, the charisma, the angry, victim, and fear messages. Ah, but he'll never get nominated. Americans are too smart for that. Oh. Shit! They nominated him. So I started sending out alarm signals on Facebook. Post after post. Obsessively. He can't win. He mustn't and here's why. Oh, the pushback I got from both some family members and some friends was awful, but I didn't care. I was NOT giving up. And then he won. God help us.

The only energy I had left was to furiously knit pink pussy hats and march with other women. They gave me hope. Then formerly resistant Republicans, one by one, started falling in line, so I started posting away again. The pushback became more ferocious. My friends weren't getting it. The nation wasn't getting it! Trump, his sycophantic Republicans, judges and officials crossed red line after red line. Nothing stopped him, even after he lost: J6. Fake electors. Stealing our nation's secrets to sell them to our enemies. Surely, I thought, this time he has finally gone too far, but no. Nothing was holding him accountable. Frustration. Do Trumpers really WANT a Hitler? Now I have my answer.

Four years later, I couldn't believe Trump won (or did he cheat?) again. Day after day, he's worse. MUCH worse. It's the full on fascist playbook on display to everyone in real time. If we thought the first four years were bad? America has seen nothing yet.

Done with Facebook, I/we need to fight in a different way. I joined Bluesky. It's a breath of fresh air: Millions of resisters. Here people are getting it. It feels like the Women's March. I follow and post to our representatives, independent journalists, writers and my own followers. I'm home!

But posting is not enough. HOW do I best fight to save and rebuild our democracy? I remembered the trim tab analogy used in strategic planning. The trim tab is a sailing term for that little rudder on the top of the bigger rudder that actually plays the bigger role in directing the boat. Metaphorically, it tells us we can be that trim tab. So we need to ask ourselves: What specific action can we each take that will have the most impact?

Each of us has strengths, and each of us cares passionately about something. Our democracy needs each and every one of those strengths to not just resist, but to aim those strengths toward the democratic cause we care about most passionately. Find a team or an organization that cares about that cause. Support them. Strategize. Act.

My strengths are skills in research and writing. My passion is election integrity. My specific action (besides posting) is that I now volunteer for a nonpartisan organization called SMART Elections. It is dedicated to researching voter data, anomalies and threats to keep our elections secure. And there is plenty of data that suggests manipulation of the vote counts. I don't know that the data can or will change the outcome, or that Trump will ever be held accountable for rigging an election, but data is not a conspiracy, and the truth must be known to protect the integrity of the next election.

My dad used to tell us, "You can either learn by example or you can learn the hard way, but either way, you will learn." Trump supporters chose the latter. When they experience the consequences of his abuses firsthand, there's hope they, too, will eventually turn against him and join the resistance. Together, we must turn the tide.

It's up to us, the people, to save our democracy. Our founding fathers stated this in the Declaration of Independence. Other countries have succeeded at stopping tyranny as well. We can and must follow their example - or learn the hard way.

Yolaine M. Stout, CFRM, ACLSC, is a descendant of four American Revolutionary soldiers. She is a 25 year veteran German and English high school teacher and an Honors graduate from UC Berkeley. She is also the founder and/or President of several nonprofits, a strategic planner and nonprofit consultant. She, and her late husband, Dr. Charles D. Stout, a renowned crystallographer, successfully sued the County of San Diego for approving a destructive development of critical habitat. They then wrote grants to raise several million dollars in order to purchase that land. It is now a nature preserve called Wright's Field that is freely used by the public. Mrs. Stout continues her work in translating, researching, volunteering and writing for causes she believes in. She is President and Founder of ACISTE and a volunteer for Smart Elections. She and her late husband raised three boys (two of whom were adopted), along with countless cats and chickens.

The Space I Inhabit

By Beatriz Terrazas

I'm not unfamiliar with rage. Soy Latina. A daughter of immigrants, and a first generation American, I am one in a never-ending line of the "otherized" in this country, despite my birthright. But after November 5th, faced with the kind of misogyny and bigotry directed at immigrants, women, trans people, and so many others by the President-elect and those who voted for him, my rage burns so strong that it eclipses any other emotions. Except for loneliness. It's hard to describe how small and disenfranchised I feel against the onslaught of so much hate.

But then, my ancestors show up. As usual, when they have something to say, their arrival is preceded by the aroma of incense, a smokiness so insistent it won't be ignored. "Listen," they demand. "Are you not one of us? Did we not survive wars and hunger? Did we not create shelter and clothing from air and dust? Did we not laugh while washing clothes in the river and love one another through the bloody nights of revolution? Did we not create you from want and hardship as an emissary of hope to a country, and a world, sorely needing it?"

They're right, of course. Resistance takes many forms, and the boldest might be the simple act of fully inhabiting the space in which we live.

Resistance is the Black man singing at the top of his voice no matter who's listening. It's the brown-skinned woman in a hijab walking her dog along the middle of the sidewalk. It's the gay man saying to his partner, "I love you," and the indigenous woman birthing a son into the land stolen from her people. This is resistance.

Living fully is resistance.

I belong. This country, which was mine before the election, is still mine. I was born here, and I grew up here. This is where I learned to read, play softball, and drive my first car. Where I received my high school diploma and university degree, and where I got my first job and apartment. I've voted in every general election and most midterms and local elections

27

for 40 years. I have paid taxes since I started working. For decades, I have served on nonprofit boards. I chair a board that provides legal aid for needy immigrants, and serve on another that seeks to connect communities with recreational trails. I buried my mother here and periodically sweep away the desert soil that gathers on the stone marking her grave.

I will continue to run and ride my bike in my North Texas neighborhood. I will open my laptop and spread my papers on the table in my local coffee shop where I meet friends. I will take my time selecting bread in the aisle of the grocery store, even if my shopping cart blocks someone for a few seconds. I will take my time settling into that airplane seat, and I will use the armrest. I will sit on a park bench and enjoy the sun on my skin. I refuse to allow the hate of others to banish me into the shadows of society.

I will be cordial, civil, and kind. But I will not cede my space.

I will still work to counteract the wrongs I see. I will still be a shoulder for the gay or pregnant teen, still speak up for the Black woman or trans man bullied on social media. You are not alone. I am not alone.

If my actions don't change the world, they will at least ensure that the world does not change me—and in those times you feel you cannot take up space, I will hold that space for you.

Beatriz Terrazas is a writer and Pulitzer Prize winning photographer with an abiding belief in the power of story to change lives. She worked as a photojournalist at the Fort Worth Star-Telegram for several years before moving to The Dallas Morning News where she covered everything from professional sports to politics, from domestic news to international stories. While there, she was part of a team of journalists who won the 1994 Pulitzer Prize for a global project that addressed the issue of violence against women through the prism of human rights. She was awarded a Nieman Fellowship in 1998, set her cameras aside for a few years, and proceeded to earn recognition for her writing, including the Gold in the Society of American Travel Writers and a first place and honorable mention in the American Society of Journalists and Authors. She was also a finalist in the James Beard Journalism Awards. Her work is included in several anthologies, the most recent being The Art of Touch, A Collection of Prose and Poetry from the Pandemic and Beyond, from the University of Georgia Press, Nov. 2023. In 2024, she was a judge for Pictures of the Year (POY), an annual, international photojournalism contest sponsor.

Why Dissent
By Carolyn Faggioni

Why do you post about politics?
You know, many people find it annoying.
You're not going to change anyone's mind.
It's a waste of time.
You will lose friends, both on and off social media.
Are things really so bad? You're being dramatic.
You're going to hurt your business.
Be careful You might trigger a violent person.

If you post about politics, as I do, you've probably heard similar things from well-intentioned family and friends.
This is my response.

I post about politics as a form of dissent.
I've written about politics for decades, long before Donald Trump was a political figure.

I've been critical of policies and politicians on both sides of the political aisle, however, as a lifelong Democrat, I tend to favor progressive policy over conservative.

The advent of social media has made the process of political advocacy easier, with publication decisions no longer solely at the mercy of editorial boards.

Nevertheless, I will continue to submit pieces to more traditional news outlets as well. When it comes to dissent, the greater the reach, the better.

While I appreciate the concern expressed by some, exercising my right to dissent is non-negotiable.
Here's why:

Dissent is patriotic.

In the United States, a nation founded with a revolution to secure liberty, dissent is woven into the very fabric of citizenship.

If one needs reminding, just take a look at the opening paragraphs of the *Declaration of Independence*, a poetic expression of social contract theory, justifying taking action in *defense of unalienable rights* and *against unjust government.*

> *We hold these truths to be self-evident, that all men are created equal, that they are endowed by their Creator with certain unalienable Rights, that among these are Life, Liberty and the pursuit of Happiness—That to secure these rights, Governments are instituted among Men, deriving their just powers from the consent of the governed,—That whenever any Form of Government becomes destructive of these ends, it is the Right of the People to alter or to abolish it, and to institute new Government, laying its foundation on such principles and organizing its powers in such form, as to them shall seem most likely to effect their Safety and Happiness.*

> *-Declaration of Independence*

Not only does the *Declaration of Independence* justify dissent, the first amendment of the *Bill of Rights* (to the United States Constitution) provides constitutional protection.

> *"Congress shall make no law… abridging the freedom of speech, or of the press; or the right of the people peaceably to assemble, and to petition the government for a redress of grievances."*

As an American concerned about the future of our democracy, I will continue to exercise my first amendment rights, including the right to free speech, freedom of the press, and the right to peacefully demonstrate, especially in support of our democratic institutions.

The notion that if one dissents they are not patriotic is nonsense.

Dissent is needed now more so than any time in recent history.

To do so is patriotic.

Dissent may be morally required.

At times, dissent is morally required, especially in support of those without a voice and without a vote.

Tragically, many groups have been disenfranchised throughout our nation's history—Native Americans, African Americans, Chinese Americans, Japanese Americans, Jewish Americans, Mexican Americans, women, Muslim Americans, and LGBTQ individuals, to name a few. (If you're thinking I'm being too harsh or not harsh enough, it is worthwhile to remember that no country is without flaws.)

Change only comes when voices are collectively raised in opposition. We've witnessed this transformative process, time and time again.

As Reverend Martin Luther King famously wrote in *A Letter from a Birmingham Jail,*

"Injustice anywhere is a threat to justice everywhere."

This nation cannot live up to its creed, expressed in its foundational documents, if good people remain silent bystanders to injustice. People of good conscience must speak out and stand up for those without a voice and vote.

Civil rights leaders relentlessly put their own freedom and security in jeopardy in order to advocate for the rights of the disenfranchised and marginalized. "Making good trouble" to dramatize injustice and bring about change, like Congressman John Lewis and countless others have done, with far too many paying the ultimate price including Medgar Evers, Malcolm X, Martin Luther King, and Robert F. Kennedy has helped to pave the way for a better future.

Given this history, the very least we can do in the face of injustice is dissent through words and actions.

Dissent is a form of creative expression, solidarity, and a core element of civil discourse.

Collective voices raised for the common good can help this nation rise.

Progressive Republican President Theodore Roosevelt had said,

"The welfare of each of us is dependent fundamentally upon the welfare of all of us".

When people come together to pursue an end that goes beyond their own narrowly defined self-interest, they are fulfilling the highest form of civic engagement.

United States Senator John McCain, who frequently emphasized the importance of service, explained,

> *"If you find faults with our country, make it a better one. If you're disappointed with the mistakes of government, join its ranks and work to correct them... Feed a hungry child. Teach an illiterate adult to read. Comfort the afflicted. Defend the rights of the oppressed. Our country will be the better, and you will be the happier. Because nothing brings greater happiness in life than to serve a cause greater than yourself."*

Being part of a movement dedicated to progressive change uplifts. We are uplifted as individuals as we discover we are not alone and there is strength in our numbers. We are energized. Society is uplifted when goals that advance the common good are achieved.

The greatest advocates for social justice throughout history understood the need for collective dissent - Mohandas Gandhi, Frederick Douglas, Sojourner Truth, Malcolm X, Nelson Mandela, and Desmond Tutu. Their words and actions have inspired generations committed to social justice and positive change.

Dissent paves the way for progress.

> *"The arc of the moral universe is long, but it bends towards justice."*
> *-Reverend Martin Luther King Jr.*

Some mistakenly think this statement means a more just society is inevitable. That couldn't be further from the truth.

As Dr. King emphasized in "A Letter from a Birmingham Jail", a more just world will only come about when people of good conscience collectively demand change.

Dissent in the face of injustice is needed to bring about change and help us come closer to that "more perfect union" that the *Preamble to the United States Constitution* promises Americans.

"We the People of the United States, in Order to form a more perfect Union, establish Justice, insure domestic Tranquility, provide for the common defense, promote the general Welfare, and secure the Blessings of Liberty to ourselves and our Posterity, do ordain and establish this Constitution for the United States of America."

Final Thoughts

I am grateful to be a citizen of a democracy and I will not take it for granted. Democracy is too precious.

Rights should not be wasted, especially first amendment rights. As I used to tell my students, the first amendment was first for a reason.

We are fortunate to reside in a democracy in which individuals are equipped with constitutionally protected liberties. When these liberties are being threatened by those that wield power, voices need to be collectively raised in opposition.

The current administration represents such a threat.

Our democracy deserves defending.

On June 14, 2025, Flag Day, President Trump has planned a military style parade, uncharacteristic of our democracy and more aligned with authoritarian regimes. The day also happens to be his birthday.

Do not allow him to abuse the symbol of our democracy in this manner.

Be part of the opposition and join a "No Kings Day" march near you!

https://www.nokings.org/

Make your voice heard! Dissent! It's patriotic! It's the right thing to do!

Carolyn Faggioni is a retired high school social studies teacher from New York State. In Carolyn's 39-year career she has taught numerous courses including Advanced Placement United States Government and Politics and World History. Carolyn is committed to defending our democracy, promoting civic engagement, and social justice. Carolyn has recently launched a newsletter Ascent with Carolyn on Substack.

Spiritual Gangsterism and the Art of Conversation
By Shane Montgomery

This morning, I walked outside and into a day that recalled my early spring lifeguard training in Corpus Christi, Texas: the dopamine-producing kind of weather edged with a chill that made the relatively warm water of the lap pool lane a womb I never wanted to leave. Though small- boned, I'd held a belief I could become strong enough to save lives. So, barely 16 yet and armed with sheer will and naivete, I powered through fatigue, aches, and the nagging doubt I could save anyone, much less myself. It wasn't me against the water; it was me against the world. On passing, I secured a job at the WASPy private club where my family had a membership. However, after getting fired one month in for not getting along with my much older narcissistic and very patriarchal (read: flirtatious) male manager, I was hired at a mostly Hispanic inner-city pool. Even at my young age, the class division was clear. These pool patrons weren't the elite Hispanic socialites in my high school inner circle, but mostly from the service sector. Yet they were families like any other: children laughing and trying to not run or hang on or near the diving boards when I blew my whistle, and parents enjoying this respite from the summer heat while keeping a close eye on their kids.

Fast forward to 2025. I still doubt I can save anyone. I'm at a loss, wandering through a dystopian minefield where, since Donald Trump's January 20th inauguration, the immigration landscape has made a shocking, seismic shift from our collective childhood dreams of saving humanity to a physical and psychological battleground of ICE conducting raids and hauling undocumented civilians out of retail and grocery stores, hospitals, schools, and churches.

Every year we celebrate wars fought to free innocents from fascism, yet we regress into a sinister, xenophobic world of mass deportation, destined to be remembered as a nation of hate, driven by the ghosts of the

Third Reich, where every dark-skinned Anne Frank without the proper papers must live and hide in fear. All that's missing are the trains. To put things in perspective, there's no mention of ICE raiding neighborhoods with large populations of Eastern European immigrants and refugees. Please read that sentence again.

Though I'd known big changes were coming, such as the immediate deportation of incarcerated gang members, I had no idea parents and children who'd crossed the US-Mexico border to escape cartel violence were being arrested and hauled off to deportation camps, until a colleague walked into the Bishop Arts District store where I'm a vendor, and announced ICE was going door-to-door along the major boulevard bordering our cluster of shops. That evening at my neighborhood mercado, tears slid down my cheeks on seeing less than a handful of people shopping in the produce section, and it dawned on me: What of the children left at home while their moms ran out for milk? The elderly? The ill? The breastfeeding babies? These aren't just immigrants; they are refugees.

Which brings me to my next point. Most American citizens, especially those on the right, have no idea that the cartels control one-third of Mexican territory, and extort small business owners on the regular; however, extortion is common in almost two-thirds of Mexico's 32 states. If people can't afford to pay, the cartel thug instructs, say, a mother to hold up her newborn, and the thug shoots the child so the flesh and blood splatters the mom. They target the children, no matter if the parents promise to pay when they can.

Many escaping the violence drown trying to cross the Rio Grande. On a more universal note, when it comes to swimming or drowning, we're all constantly fighting some current. As for me, when I want to give up and sink to the bottom, I remember how to power through the pain, and search for answers as to how we might manifest a functional and more humanitarian society, not by focusing on the surface-level high concept, but by diving into the depths.

In a microcosmic sense, I've found one such pathway to resist the fascist hive-mind mentality is through reconciliation and healing. I source art, antiques, and vintage clothing at a giant warehouse where people from all backgrounds and ethnicities work together and get along. I'd be lying if I didn't say it was a family of sorts, with many hugs and stories exchanged. My friends from Mexico, Central and South America are scared, with many making plans to leave. My Black friends are frightened, too, as they feel certain they're next on the culling list. Unsurprisingly, my white friends from Eastern Europe feel safely grandfathered in because of skin—an argument as fallacious as the one about trusting someone in office-clothes. I've lied to people in a pencil skirt and heels. I found the truth while wearing rags in the desert. However, stereotypes of an external nature are only one metric to consider.

An older white lady, ironically named Karen, was aghast that I failed to see how this mass deportation and uprooting of lives might be necessary. I calmly explained the horrendous cartel economy and how that works, reminding her if she were in their shoes, she'd swim as fast as she could across the Rio Grande. She told me she couldn't respect my stance, but that she'd never had more respect for me than when I would rescue dogs and save them from animal service's death row. She said, "I really like you, then." I shared the story of my non-English-speaking next-door neighbors saving and welcoming into their family three-legged and one-eyed dogs who'd been hit by cars and abandoned. Her expression flowered into something beautiful. A few minutes later, she announced, "Well, I'm fiscally conservative but socially liberal." She had, after all, held a management position at a major bank for years. With a mixture of awe and wonder on her face, she smiled and said, "Wow, we're on opposite sides, yet we just had a conversation." I smiled and replied gently, "Yes. We did."

Resistance, Respect and Hope
By Stephanie Ackerman

The room is filled with anxious faces, students squirming in their seats, too shy and afraid to meet my gaze. I begin my workshop by encouraging them that they have a right to higher education, to change their lives, and to be the first in their families to go to college.

Many of the students have parents who don't speak English. Several have "birthright citizenship." Most work after school or care for younger siblings. They question how their families will get by without the added financial contribution from their jobs. A few go by "they" and not he or she. Each student has a distinctive story and each has a desire to better their lives. Yet, despite the optimism in the workshop, there is the smell of fear. They fear what will happen in their small, diverse, hardworking community. They have heard stories about ICE entering businesses and schools in New Jersey and other areas of the country.

I am an Independent Educational Consultant and I volunteer as a mentor and advisor to a community-based organization that works cooperatively with the local high school, businesses and many volunteers to ensure the success of this next generation. The students who participate in this program and their families are industrious community members who came to the United States for a better life and to access educational opportunities.

Changes in college admissions have run the gamut from test-optional policies, to the Supreme Court decision not to allow colleges to see ethnic background questions on the Common Application, to the dismantling of DEI offices on campus. Students need to consider their bodies and their right to choose when selecting where they want to attend college. What is the climate for healthcare, peaceful protests, and access to advanced placement tests? (Florida does not allow the AP African American Studies course as part of the curriculum, claiming it is against

State law) Underrepresented students are afraid to fill out the Federal Student Aid Forms. (FAFSA)

What can I do? I resist. I refuse to give up on a student because of the color of their skin, the language their parents speak, their sexuality or gender. I support and guide them and let them know that there are Americans who want them to succeed. There are neighbors who fight for their rights to remain in the community and get a good education and I will continue to mentor, teach and value the adults they will become.

Stephanie Ackerman received her Bachelor of Arts degree from Hampshire College and a Master of Arts from Brandeis University. For two years, she served as the Admissions Chair of the Parents Council for Elon University, overseeing admissions initiatives with yield events, recruiting, summer welcome events, and working with admissions counselors, students, and families around the country. In addition to owning her computer training business working with children, teens, adults, and companies, she was the technology director/instructor in a private K-8 school. Stephanie volunteered with JBJ's Soul Kitchen Employment and Empowerment Team as a career coach.

Her professional memberships include; the Independent Educational Consultants Association (IECA) Professional Member, New Jersey IECA Professional Member, and the New Jersey Association of College Admissions Counselors. (NJACAC) She received her certificate as an Independent College Admissions Consultant from the University of California-San Diego, June 2019.

How Do We Trust in a Broligarchy?
By A. M. Carley

It's intense out there. Incompetence, deceit, bad actors, and misinformation campaigns surround us. The risks are greater all the time with advances in AI. Will we humans form a resistance movement to maintain personal connections in a world where AI, owned and operated by the broligarchy, wants us to give their targeted propaganda more credibility than our own direct experience?

Is reliance only for the gullible?

When I was in law school in the 80s, my Contracts professor—I'll call him Hut—scorned the legal concept of "reliance." Hut (think Dr. House, but a generation older and more disreputable looking) implied that anyone gullible enough to change their behavior based on promises made by another deserved the mess that might result. Hut gave us hypothetical cases: Abel offers to sell Zadie his handcrafted guitar in one month. She excitedly agrees, and signs up for a pricey intensive guitar course right away, to get ready.

When Abel reneges and secretly sells his guitar the next day for more money, Zadie has wasted her cash on the course. If she takes Abel to court, she might request "reliance damages," to reimburse her for the money she spent on the now-pointless guitar course. Professor Hut would call BS and say Zadie was a fool for believing Abel and relying on his promise; she deserved nothing from him. The Nanny State would be escorting fine upstanding Americans to hell in a handcart if we supported reliance damages. That was Hut's take. At the time, his attitude offended my beliefs that people are good at heart and we should look out for one another.

I gathered Hut was a skeptic by nature, and that life had confirmed his lowest expectations. The man was regularly spotted day-drinking at a nearby tavern, he reeked of cigarette smoke, wore wrinkled suit jackets that hung on his skeletal frame, and looked out at the world with droopy basset-hound eyes in a lined, mournful face. No accident, then, that I think of Hut when I ponder the near future. The days of naïve reliance are behind us—all of us.

Now more than ever, people can't be counted on to do the right thing. Those like me, who, last November, harbored a faint hope that new, younger energy might correct the course of the ship of State, are regrouping and pondering how to be.

Trustworthy people

Who's at the helm? Not just of the federal government, but all the many nongovernmental positions of authority that help make things happen? People in charge of utilities, banks, grocery stores, pharmaceutical companies, insurers, schools. Booking agents, concert impresarios, publishers, museum directors, literary agents? It behooves us to do our research each time we want to interact in the world.

Will we writers send out pitches for articles to people and publications with whom we have no human connection? Maybe not so much. If a friend of a relative of a colleague knows someone with an online publication, I'm likely to feel okay about dropping them a line with an idea for an essay. On the other hand, if the literary agent I saw pop up on social media recently sounds bogus, they might be a bot—not even a human, let alone a trustworthy agent. It will be on me to dig around and see whether the agent is query-worthy. Or real. My community will matter more to me, and I may feel the need to expand it.

Trustworthy information

What will we trust now? So much online is not reliably genuine: text may be bot-generated. Images and videos may be fabricated ineptly by AI. (See three-armed yogis, chunks of frozen salmon swimming upstream, etc.) We must stay on our toes and use discernment. Which environments are more likely to be trustworthy

Friends are backing away from all social media—although I've been advised it's prudent to park your accounts, leaving the name and some placeholder data, rather than deleting them altogether. Your name and identity on that platform could be hijacked if you delete your account entirely. Others are subscribing to newly formed news media outlets, canceling their subscriptions to traditional print and online media and revising their broadcast and podcast habits. We'll need to keep our eyes and ears open—this won't be a one-and-done alteration in habits—and the information landscape will continue to shift.

What steps will you not take any more? Some refuse to shop with the Seattle-based megavendor. Others look up the ratios between a company's CEO pay and its median employee salary, and look to confirm the existence of a robust DEI policy before choosing where they'll make their next purchases. When ads for pumpkin-shaped potholders show up moments after you conducted a search for them online, you may look around for a newer, less gossipy search engine.

For myself, I'm warming to a series of challenges. Maybe I can organize an online meeting of some writers I know. Maybe I can invite more writers to contribute guest posts to my blog. Maybe I can be bolder about approaching new creative people who are legitimately connected to those I know now. At the end of a novel I'm completing, the protagonist begins collaborating in multigenerational artistic endeavors. Might that happen in real life too?

Isolation is not an option

The supposed grownups in charge can't be trusted to overcome their apparently feral impulses, prejudices, disrespect, greed, and contempt for the rest of humanity. A voice from the back of the cave murmurs: "Just stay home. Leave the activism to others."

But isolation doesn't work. We're primates who require interaction. So going forward, I'll be doing more thinking ahead: Connecting with humans I can vouch for. Seeing what small actions I can take, locally or in trusted groups online, to have a positive impact about issues that matter to me. I'm gravitating toward a sense of belonging.

Planning in community

We'll be doing more planning and less flying by the seat of our pants—at least most of the time. We may still get crazy sometimes, and fling caution aside in favor of the feeling of freedom. For the next while, though, daily life is going to feel more buttoned-down. As a consequence, creative practices are going to be even more important for us all. More than ever, we'll want to focus on doing what we do well and get into that state of flow where we can operate outside of the everyday.

What does this add up to?

Find your people. Identify and monitor your trusted information sources. Support one another with kindness, attribution, and cash. Foster your creative practice. And keep hope alive through focused action, starting small.

Note: A version of this essay first appeared on the Anne Carley Creative blog. https://annecarleycreative.com/2025/01/15/how-do-we-trust-in-a-broligarchy/

A M (Anne) Carley is a writer and creativity coach at annecarleycreative.com. Her handbook, *FLOAT: Becoming Unstuck for Writers*, provides empathetic interventions for writers and others who work with words. Anne believes that resistance starts at home.

Independent Publishing is Resistance
By Ilan Stavans

(Editor's note: This essay was adapted from an appeal that Stavans sent out to readers and supporters)

Queridos Amigos,

I am incensed, and likely you are too. A nation's government ought to provide the means for its citizens to engage in open, democratic debate, not handcuff them for failure to fall in line with the commander-in-chief.

I write with an urgent appeal. You will have read by now about the new administration's focus on defunding the National Endowment for the Arts, the National Endowment for the Humanities, and the Institute of Museum and Library Sciences, not to mention destroying our deeply American ethos of celebrating diverse voices, building a democratic and equitable society—I could go on. What you may not know is that the majority of independent literary presses and journals, community-focused arts organizations, individual artists and translators, and many others rely on funding from the NEA to do the work that they do.

Restless Books is one of those organizations. We rely on an annual grant of $30,000 from the NEA to publish our books each year; without it, those books are in jeopardy. Fewer books would be a victory for Trump, who thrives on chaos and retribution, and hopes to silence diverse writers. Now more than ever, I'm convinced these stories must be told—without federal dollars if necessary. Neither this nor any other president should dictate what we read—not in a representative democracy. Our republic of readers, national and global, is stronger than the politicians who fear them. Politics for Trump is the art of the deal. But art is much more: free, revealing, impassioned, surprising. And so I turn to you. I need your support.

The National Endowment for the Arts was not created with Republican or Democratic money. It is funded by taxpayers and approved by Congress. As the cofounder and publisher of Restless Books, I have always been careful not to politicize our endeavor, instead allowing the works we support to speak for themselves. It is readers who must find meaning in our books, not the government.

But when I found out that the NEA was being defunded, I wrote a public response. Restless also filed a formal appeal. And I did something else: I personally sent President Trump two of our books: *How Yiddish Changed America and How America Changed Yiddish* (2020) and *The People's Tongue: Americans and the English Language* (2023), the first dealing with the contribution of Jews in America, the second exploring the ways people reinvent English and vice versa. Both books display opposing opinions, which I think is always useful in the art of reasoning. I don't know if Trump will actually get the books, let alone read them. But books are what matter to me: more than a writer, I'm a reader. I hope the president can be a reader, too.

This month, as the staff of Restless Books looks ahead to our 2026 publication calendar, we're wondering if we will still be able to publish the 11 titles we had planned, with the various details—full-color illustrations for some, hardcover presentation for others, successful publicity campaigns for all—that can make the difference for a book in translation.

I'm an immigrant from Mexico. I'm also a Jew. What Donald Trump is doing with America is tragic. Some intellectual and artistic heavyweights have announced they are leaving the United States. I'm nobody's judge. Yet if there was ever a time to be here, fighting for our First Amendment rights and cherished democratic principles, this is it. That fight must take many forms, from speaking out in the face of repression to acts of kindness. Our duty is to remain passionate, informed citizens. And yes, to read as broadly as possible, not only writers and opinions you agree with but—even more importantly—those you disagree with. Intolerance must be fought with openness.

Please help. And yes, read, read, read

Muchas gracias,
Ilan Stavans

Ilan Stavans is a Mexican-born Jewish-American writer and academic. He writes and speaks on American, Hispanic, and Jewish cultures. He is the author of *Quixote* and a contributor to the *Norton Anthology of Latino Literature*.

Words Matter

By Anna Tambour

We've got to tackle the new euphemisms though they're slipperier than KY Lube.

Euph: Questionable Legality

Meaning: Illegal. So fucking illegal, we're scared to say so.

Euph: DOGE official, DOGE staffer, DOGE employee

Meaning: Muskultist thug, cyberterrorist, unlisted America's (and Putin's and Xi's) most wanted.

A young person needed by Musk to carry out his ends. Employee? Of what or whom? Not the government that he's acting against, as an enemy recruit. Musk's and Trump's attitude toward labor is laughable. Most likely, this dupe has been paid nothing, but will surely pay for his actions for the rest of his life.

There is no such thing as a "DOGE staffer." "Staff" presumes there's something real to staff. DOGE is a wholly illegal terror gang given a fancy name by Trump, a felon himself, to pay a megadonor who expects to rule everything and have the country pay for it, and has got Trump by his smelly curlies.

The little band of Muskutists are terrorists, pure and simple, and he's done more—aided by Trump—than Osama Bin Laden could ever have dreamed.

Euph: Common Sense

Meaning: It's Trump's fave new reason for everything from ethnic cleansing to blaming DEI for a plane crash.

Euph: Alternative Facts

Kelly Anne Conway's attempt to cover Trump with the phrase "alternative facts" was merely funny, but the *New York Times* and *Washington Post* have lost more subscribers than Trump has hair, from their practice of grabbing more fat phrases and multisyllabic gallumps for "lie" than state fair goers do fried foods.

Antidemocratic governments love euphemisms that hide what's truly happening, and there are repugnant plans for more. "Resettlement to the East" inspired Trump's "beautiful" new plan for Palestinians. "Arbeit macht frei", the German phrase" work will make you free" above the camp gates of Auschwitz, must have inspired Musk's "Work like hell." Propaganda depends on words that mean the opposite, convey threat without coming out and threatening, and enforce obeisance.

When media self-censors and tailors language to fit those who should be fought, and acts as a cooperative force, it is an antisocial act that needs and will be swept away, just as leaders have been who crush people, throughout history. Words matter so much that in 2014, China banned puns because of one making gentle fun of Xi. The announced reason for the ban was that punning "violates China's cultural tradition," but political puns are, indeed, the opposite—a centuries-long tradition which has existed as long as there has been repression.

We can use words, too. We need honesty and precision, first of all. But we also need words as cartoon rapiers. It's hard now to laugh at what's happening, but to combat demagogues we need good laughs. Laughter is surprisingly powerful against those raping and pillaging the world. They have such thin skin that it can put them into an unhealthy situation to hear or see their own words tossed back at them.

Anna Tambour is a writer. Last novel, *Smoke Paper Mirrors: a short saga for our times.* Last collection: *Death Goes to the Dogs.* She lives in Australia.

Translating Obfuscation
By Ryk E. Spoor

I'm a Science Fiction/Fantasy author by preference and avocation, but I'm a writer of technical proposals, reports, manuals, and such by profession. My wife Kathleen has always been more of an activist—I dislike confrontation and I am often, even when I'm 99% sure I'm right, hesitant to talk about political issues because I'm afraid I'm just plain wrong.

But with the emergence of Trump and his increasingly unhinged followers, I felt I had to do *something*. But I didn't have time or resources to spare for a lot of things, so what could I do?

And then I heard about Project 2025. After several mentions, I decided I really ought to take a look at this thing. So I did… and made a surprising (to me) discovery:

This 900+ page document *was a technical proposal*. It was written in the same language, with the same purposes, as the stuff I'd been working on for 23+ years. That included the phrasing to avoid saying things you didn't want the reader to hear—while not leaving the key information out; the way you present unpalatable truths in the most pleasant manner for the audience, the approach used to lead the reader to the specific conclusion you want, while not letting them see what you're hiding.

But it was a *massive* proposal, written by consummate professionals, deliberately crafted to a specific audience and phrased to cover up the pure distilled virulence of the ideas. And while people were posting alerts on some of the pieces of the document, they were usually referring to page numbers—which could be easily changed.

And so I realized what I could do… was go through the whole thing, page by page, *quote* key parts (rather than simply refer to page numbers), and distill *ALL* of it into summaries of what was *really* being said, of what the authors truly intended to accomplish, and—perhaps most importantly—to constantly point to how all of it was interrelated, part of a single, carefully-worked-out plan of action.

So I started posting each day my interpretation of each section of the Project as I read them. To my surprise, people *did* read those posts—and some started passing them around. In the end, I gathered all of them into a single document (itself around 150 pages—there's only so much you can distill), and it turned out a number of people wanted a copy, including some of the political organizations out there.

That reaction—knowing people found that helpful—is what keeps me posting more updates, every week, on the current slew of catastrophes; I call these posts, perhaps with a bit too much deprecation, "rants," but it's what I can do: draw attention to lies I hear, pick apart the delusional assertions the far Elon Right wants us to believe, and, when I encounter it, to translate political and legal language into the actual meaning that they're trying to hide.

Each of us have talents that can be used to educate, to fight, to hold the line. Kathleen has artistic talent and vision, and that's her weapon.

Me, I'm a writer. And as a writer, I will not allow them to use language to conceal evil.

Ryk E. Spoor is an American science fiction and fantasy author, who also writes research grant proposals for a technology firm. He published his first novel, Digital Knight, in 2003, and has gone on to publish over a dozen more novels, often in collaboration with author Eric Flint on their Boundary series

Acts of Resistance During the War on Transgender
By Riki Wilchins

As transgender people, and especially the rights of trans kids. have come under unprecedented legislative and political assault in 26 states to date and now directly from the White House itself, every day resistance has become more important than ever.

Some of what we're doing is basic old-school activism: calling our elected representatives, joining the ACLU, Lambda Legal, or the National Center for Women's Rights, joining the legal groups who are criss-crossing the country, filing scores of lawsuits in the fight against MAGA state laws and Trump's anti-trans Executive Orders.

Other acts are more subtle. Many of the most important assaults have attacked trans people's access to gender-affirming medical care. In my own case, that's meant getting my Vitamin E (i.e., estrogen) on the annual vacations my wife and I take to Cartagena, which is just a two-hour flight away from Florida—where our Trump-wannabee governor has made hormones for trans teens illegal, and, for adults, increasingly difficult to get.

Another Red state friend of mine who has family in Mexico City has them smuggle in his hormones when they come to visit. He tongue-in-check refers to them as his "testosterone mules."

Parents with trans kids trapped in Red states by jobs or homes can't make regular trips up north to a Blue state where puberty blockers or hormones are legal, and they have to stock up whenever their trans teen runs low, when they can manage a visit north. Others in blue states are sending money to help families buy affirming medication for their kids, or buying and stockpiling the medications themselves and mailing them to friends in Red states, which is now illegal if they're caught.

Over 100,000 trans people and affirming families have fled Red states in the last two years. It is an unprecedented internal displacement of political refugees that is without precedent in modern American history. Often with little money, they need places to stay. There's a kind of transgender underground railroad of people willing to put them up for a night or two on their way to a safer state, perhaps even one of the three sanctuary states that promises to ignore out-of-state subpoenas on trans issues.

In the late 1990s we had a street-action group, The Transexual Menace, which protested in cities all over the country when trans people were killed. Then the idea fell out of favor under Obama. But times change, and trans people are once again protesting their treatment in major cities where hospitals have backed away from affirming care.

This Spring we're planning a Lobby Day on Capitol Hill to tell the Democrats face-to-face that we don't appreciate being blamed for Kamala Harris's loss, and don't appreciate them rolling over in the face of escalating Republican attempts to scapegoat us.

At a time when social media has inundated all of us every day with an endless stream of rage-bait, click-bait, disinformation, and snarks, one of my acts has been to stop adding to it. Instead, every day I post a news-only feed on BlueSky of two to three breaking transgender stories: no hyperbole, no anger, no sarcasm. Just 240 characters of hard news with whatever context space allows.

Some acts of every day resistance come under the title of self-care and other-care: tuning out the spin-cycle of constant head-fake news, working out regularly and getting that extra hour of sleep, checking in on trans folks you know who are emotionally vulnerable and struggling, offering to help those in need, and reminding everyone to rest and sleep and that we will get through this. Try as they might, you can't just wipe one million Americans away. We have always survived, and we will survive this.

Not every act of resistance is every day; some are quite extraordinary. For my book *When Loving Your Kids is a Crime,* I interviewed a Texas mom who was informed by her Lambda lawyer that the Department of Family Services was about to get aggressive in its open investigation of her and her transgender daughter.

With the closest state border already mapped out, she loaded her three kids—one trans, one autistic, two cats and three lizards into their beat-up van within hours, driving for four days and nights to the closet sanctuary state. There they spent long winter weeks living out of the van in Connecticut. She'd drop the kids off at school during the day and deliver packages for Walmart so they had gas and food. At night she'd park at a truck stop out on the interstate and they'd recline in their seats and watch Netflix until sleep came. Every week or so, someone would pay for a hotel room so they could bathe, sleep in a real bed, and have warm food from the microwave.

I think of her and her kids—they were so afraid that they moved from Connecticut, a sanctuary state, to Scotland—when I consider my own struggles here and what so many of us go through. I remind myself that these things come in cycles and if I can just find ways to resist this one it will end in four years and something else will take its place. .

But mostly I remind myself that survival itself is a kind of resistance. Because you can take away my pronouns, my passport, my prison cell, my hormones, and my bathroom, I'm still trans. I'm still here. I'm not going anywhere. And tomorrow there will are only going to be more of me. I'm not scared, I'm fighting mad. You can't have my life: it's mine. Because we are the future of what gender looks like.

Riki Wilchins has 25 years of writing, advocacy, and research on gender and trans issues. She is a founder of the first national transgender advocacy group, GenderPAC, as well as the direct action group The Transexual Menace [sic]. Riki is the author of seven books on gender theory and politics, and her writing has appeared in popular media outlets *The Village Voice* and *Social Text*, peer review publications such as *The Journal of Research on Adolescence* and *The Journal of Homosexuality*, and also her own recurring blog at Medium.com/@rikiwilchins. She has conducted gender trainings for institutions including the White House, CDC, and the HHS Office on Women's Health. Riki's work has been profiled by *The New York Times. TIME* magazine selected Riki among "100 Civic Innovators for the 21st Century." She lives in sunny South Beach with her partner, one daughter, two dogs, and three tennis racquets.

Nine Ways to Keep From Going Crazy for Four Years of the Trump Fiasco
By Perry Brass

1) Take Trump seriously, but don't believe a word he says. Or, for your own sanity, believe, say, every third word. Trump is a pathological liar. He really has bought most of his own lies, so at this point he firmly believes his own lies to be the truth. The best example of this are his lies about January 6, 2021, which he now believes was done by loving, patriotic, kind tourists to the Capitol.

2) 2Expect a lot of conservative blow-back regarding immigration, same-sex marriage and relationships, inflation, and civil safety, among other issues and problems. Also, make room in your own beliefs for the opinions of others in the US. This does not mean you believe these opinions to be the "gospel" truth, but try to understand where they are coming from, and, if possible, think about how your own beliefs can bring theirs in. Most progressives do believe in the basic goodness of humans, their desire for justice and genuine decency—decency meaning treating other people with a moral imperative to consider their welfare as well as your own

 You can use these beliefs when thinking and talking about immigration, same-sex marriage, etc.

3) Do everything you can to keep yourself safe, and not alienated and alone. This means get off your screens and make real relationships with people. Humans need each other, and during pressing difficult times we need one another more. So work at deeper friendships and relationships—work towards not just people you "date," but people you will genuinely love. These people don't have to agree with you 100%, but with them you should feel a deeper sense of emotional and physical safety than you would alone.

4) Give money, time, effort, and energy to local and national politicians you feel represent your ideals, ideas, desires, and actions. People in America have a knee-jerk disdain for politics, which is a great thing to have, if you want to enable a fascist take-over. When people jump, en masse, out of politics, you have what is called a "vacuum of power." This means that any asshole can jump in and grab that power. We see this in Congress all the time, thank you Margery Taylor Greene and her ilk. If you want smart, rational government that means working with smart, rational politicians. They are out there, and you can find them.

5) Keep yourself as fit as possible, no matter how old you are or how unfit you have been. Your body is the house you live in, and having it go to hell during the next four years of Trump politics will make you feel even worse, more rejected and depressed. Pay attention to your diet, and how much rest and exercise you get. Also, pay attention to your finances. Being financially fit is a good idea now because there is no telling where Trump's policies will lead the country financially, unless of course you are in the Upper 0.0001 percent.

6) If you believe in a "Higher Power," fine. But don't think God is going to help us. Only we can. There are progressive religious groups, and I am all for them. Trump, who proudly wears "sin" like women used to wear mink, has been great at garnering the arch-conservative Christian rightwing vote. What this means is that people outside the Christian right must leave religion as an organizing factor and find their own means of organization, such as ecology and the Earth itself. You can leave Heaven to the right wing. We want to save the Earth. Afterall, so far it's the only place we have to live in.

7) Pay close attention to the news, but temper it with attention to who is saying what. Just because someone is saying something that sounds meaningful or possibly important, doesn't mean they really feel or mean it. When I was involved in radical gay politics in the late 1960s and early 1970s, through the Gay Liberation Front, we used to say: "Pay more attention to who is saying what than to what they are saying." In other words, Trump will say anything to sell himself (which he's good at) and his followers will do likewise. So realize the source from which all these words come.

53

8) But also allow some room to be interested in the sincerity of his followers. They may be misled, but they are sincere in their feelings. When progressives discount the sincerity of their opponents, they are already placing themselves on those dangerous ice flows leading to that place where you fall off the Earth. You may not like their sincerity, but it's theirs—and you need to take it very seriously.

9) Finally, realize we will get through this, and learn a lot from it. Life in America and democracy itself has never been the tasty Technicolor picnic the marketers want us to believe it is. This has always been the richest country in the world, and it is tempting to grab all the power and bucks you can. We now have a harsh and threatening inequality of income and resources—Trump is banking on using this inequality while at the same time contributing to it. Don't subscribe to the winner-take-all mentality. Fight for real equality and work to find resolutions for injustice. And keep your eyes and ears wide open for the next four years.

Perry Brass has published 23 books ranging from science fiction, short fiction, and "how to" books to poetry. He is the president of the Gay Liberation Front Foundation, a nonprofit dedicated to preserving the legacy of the Gay Liberation Front, the first, most radical, and influential LGBTQ organization to be formed after the Stonewall Rebellion. (glf-foundation.org) He is also a founding coordinator of the Rainbow Book Fair, the largest LGBTQ book event in the US. He can be reached through Facebook or www.perrybrass.com.

The Artist Salon: A Tradition of Resistance
By Mike Coleman

The 2020 and 2021 Democratic political victories were like the amped-up pop of a champagne cork for many of us, especially in my home state of Georgia. The "Blue Wave" delivered electoral college votes for Joe Biden and elected Jon Ossoff and Rev. Raphael Warnock to secure a Democratic Senate majority.

"Georgia saved the country," we claimed—and indeed, the corks kept popping.

Sadly, the champagne went flat on November 5, 2024.

With the crushing 2024 presidential and congressional results, what had appeared to be a Blue revolution to reshape our country's future proved to be only a ripple against the rising tide of Red retribution engulfing us all.

It's easy to feel defeated, to consider moving to Spain, Portugal, Canada—to live anywhere but here.

Such drastic action isn't possible for many of us, however. Jobs, family commitments, ties we can't imagine severing with church, friends, neighborhoods we love tether us to our homes. Besides, one can make a compelling argument that this is not the time to scatter, not the time for a Blue Diaspora. Instead, it's time for like-minded individuals to find new ways to connect, form new communities that support and nurture one another.

I've found such a community in Atlanta.

We're a small group. Small but mighty, we like to say: Five published authors of fiction and non-fiction. A musician who sings with a local Americana band. An accomplished storyteller. A painter, illustrator and historic preservationist working against Atlanta's prevailing "tear it down and build something new" approach to urban growth.

The diversity qualifies us to call ourselves an "artist salon." We're proud of that. We've named it M'ville, short for Marthasville, the second name of three for the city of Atlanta. It's a nod to the city's history and to Martha Lumpkin, the daughter of Wilson Lumpkin, Georgia's governor when the town was incorporated in 1842.

We like how the term "artist salon" lifts us above the political fray. We are not a political group, though we do stand for opening eyes and ears, and providing fresh perspectives on the culture around us.

As an artist salon, M'ville taps into the rich history of salons across the centuries. In the late 19th Century the Impressionists worked to shatter traditional definitions of art. In the early 20th Century American expat Gertrude Stein started a salon on the "Street of Flowers" in Paris that included Picasso, Hemingway, Fitzgerald—a group that is the prototype of an artist salon, as we hear the term today.

But you don't have to live in Paris to have a salon.

When I was a young newspaper reporter in Montgomery, Alabama, in the mid-1970s, I was invited to a Saturday salon at the home of Virginia Durr, who helped bail Rosa Parks out of jail and was one of the key supporters of the bus boycott in the 1950s. Besides an array of local progressive thinkers, who should be in attendance but author Jessica Mitford? Known as "Decca" to her long-time friend Virginia, liberal-minded Jessica (definitely not her fascist-leaning sister Unity) was the author of *The American Way of Death*, an exposé of the funeral industry. In my early 20's, I was awed by the impressive company, light-headed from the whiskey sours served in the heat of the midday Alabama summer sun. But I also remember a distinct feeling of belonging, of having "found my tribe," as we say today.

I've found my tribe again with M'ville.

The salon has been a source of continuous support since November 5. We gather for dinner occasionally, and keep a lively chat going on Facebook Messenger. We mentor each other on current and potential projects.

And sometimes during the tough, stressful months since the election, the salon has kept me from weeping. Kept my chin up.

We share the joy of friendship, sure. But we also share the joy of knowing that we are friends with a purpose—a common passion. Our friendship has a reason, if you will, a drive that keeps us looking forward.

Recently, we had our first "coming out."

We hosted a free, open-to-the-public salon party, a December Sunday afternoon event at a local distillery where our musician and her band performed, our illustrator offered original holiday cards for sale, and our authors presented a panel-style discussion about the writing life.

A local indie bookseller was on hand, too, selling our books, which range from Southern Gothic fiction, a mosaic novel built of connected stories about a family's hardscrabble life in rural Missouri in the 1980s, a coming-out memoir, and histories of two Atlanta institutions—the beloved Rich's department store and Westview Cemetery.

We had a great turnout. People engaged, asked questions, bought books and cards. Bought drinks, too. The distillery's bartender created a special cocktail for the occasion, called, appropriately, The Bitter Bitch

Politics were not discussed. That wasn't the point. But by creating a gathering different from football-watching or a trip to the multiplex to see the latest blockbuster release, we did something important, something that can help change worldviews.

Put another way, it was everyday resistance in action.

As I wrote this essay the morning of January 9, 2025, I clicked on a link that a fellow M'viller sent me a few weeks ago, a story about the early days of Greenwich Village featured in an exhibition at The New York Public Library. The exhibition chronicles the origin of America's first large-scale countercultural enclave on the eve of WWI when dissent was growing over outdated, 19th Century social norms. The exhibit includes a mock Declaration of Independence from January 23, 1917, when artists, actors, and poets tied red balloons from the top of the arch in Washington Square at the heart of Greenwich Village. They read aloud from the document announcing the Village's secession from the United States.

I doubt our group will ever write a Declaration of Independence and announce our secession from the US. But that red balloon spirit is alive and well in M'ville, and for now, during these frightening days, it is enough.

Mike Coleman is the winner of a 2024 Georgia Author of the Year Award for his coming-out memoir, *The Way from Me to Us*. He was recognized in 2025 by the Georgia State House of Representatives for his work.

Published by Riverdale Avenue Books in 2023, his book has won numerous accolades for its candor and emotional power. Mike has held readings and signings at bookstores and literary events in New York, Florida, Alabama, South Carolina and Georgia.

He and his husband Ted have been partners for nearly 50 years and were legally married in 2013. Read about their life together and their frequent travels at www.mikecolemanauthor.com.

Hope Blossoms in the Dark
By D. F. Jester

I was a firefighter/paramedic for 23 years. In all that time I was part of something bigger than me. I participated in public service. I felt part of a larger whole. I knew, every day, going into work could be my last day. Yet every day I did it without fear of death or injury. I have reflected back on this, and wondered how I found this kind of fortitude. I find myself realizing that the fear I did have was of failing those who I served, or of failing the people who relied on me. It was part of being something bigger than myself that reduced my selfishness, and replaced it with selflessness. So resist the tide of selfishness that is coming in.

Resist.

Stand unwavering upon your feet, and brace yourself against the incoming tide. Even as sand slips out from beneath you, and with each incoming wave your feet sink deeper into the wet sand, you must stand strong and resilient. Stay your ground and defend your convictions, even after you are pulled out, and fight against the undertow. When it feels most helpless, and you only have the strength to tread water, let your beliefs buoy you.

Fight against the riptide with your last breath. When you feel it is too much, and you want to stop and give up, that is when you must find your inner strength. And when you drift languidly beneath the lolling oceans swells, succumbing to the dark depths of the murky below, that is when you must fight hardest.

I, for one, will not drop to my knees in supplication. I will stand and resist. To do this, though, I must take a moral inventory of who I am, and what I am capable of. To resist I must first understand what I stand for, and how far I am willing to defend that position. I must examine my scruples, and decide, am I strong enough to defend those if they cannot defend themselves?

Persevere.

I will persevere. This is an act of resistance: to stand, every day, and go out into the world and do a little good. To look outside myself and do something for those who need it the most. To bring a little happiness, a little bright light for those who dwell in the dark. This will be one part of my resistance.

Participate.

As we navigate this next administration and the policies they seek to impose to alter the fabric of our democracy, I will remain resilient through my participation. I will not shrink back into the shadows when I must stand and justify my beliefs. Instead I will remain bolstered by them, wear them like armor to protect me from insidious intentions of a regime that seeks to drive us into the depths of amorality. I will stop believing that scrolling and posting is an effective method of resistance, and instead I will stand up, bodily, and march on, engaging in civics, social work, and non-profit volunteerism. When a need arises, I will do my best to give something of myself to it. My empathy will be refreshed by my participation; it will refuel my need to battle injustice.

Inspire.

I will be an inspiration. Saying you support something, posting you support something, without action isn't support, those are only words. Walk out there and inspire those around you. Give them strength through your own strength. Show those who need a shepherd that you will guide them. I know from my career that the best leaders don't order or tell you what to do, they act and you follow. Do as you say, and maybe we all will show others that we can achieve something.

I've heard the words, "Night is always darkest before dawn." I believe night will be darkest for the next four years. And that is why I will be a beacon in the dark for those who need hope. Hope will not die in the dark quietly. Hope will only die with you and me if we allow it to fade, if we choose to let it flicker in the wan, fading grey that is the dusk of despair or despondency. I won't let hope dissolve. No. I will resist until my eyes no longer behold the sun rising and bathing the world in golden light.

I will not rage. I will not succumb to anger. I will bring hope to those who need it. I will bring light where it is needed. I will stand against the incoming tide, and allow my convictions to shield me from apathy.

Every day, I will stand by my convictions. I will endure.

I will not stand idly by and be passive. I will participate. I won't let the loudest person dictate our direction. I will strive to become louder than they are.

I once wrote, "Happiness is a star you swallow whole. It becomes part of you, deep inside you, and shines bright when you open your mouth. When you stare, your eyes become phosphorescent. When you touch, beams of starlight shoot from your fingertips. Be eccentric! Embrace your idiosyncrasies. Be whimsical. Take a moment to stop and observe the good and the bad, the revolting and the pleasant, the beautiful and the ugly. Our lives are filled with juxtapositions, illustrious contrasts hidden in plain sight, ignored by so many. Sometimes in chaos we find the most beauty. Don't close your eyes, don't go underground, be ever present."

I wrote that going into 2017. Eight years later, I have something more to add.

Consume that star and be a bright fucking light in a dark world. Be the beacon for good people to rally to. And for fuck sakes, don't give up. Participate! Please, participate in something. I for one won't retreat into myself, I won't kneel for defeat. That, in it of itself, is an act of rebellion. We must remember this, hope is only lost if we let it be.

D.F. Jester is a writer and filmmaker who loves the surreal and absurd; finding life is truly stranger than fiction. His most recent film was an adaptation of the Stephen King short story, One For The Road, and he has a story in an upcoming horror anthology. When he is not writing, filming, or reading, he is trekking across foreign lands on tiny motorbikes that were never conceived to be driven in the conditions he subjects them to.

Resisting the Old White Fear
By Shane Montgomery

I resist what I've coined "The Old White Fear," both in my writing and in my actions toward others. I consider myself a word warrior, my best battles fought on the page in a lifelong crusade against patriarchal constructs and subsequent societal injustices, including -but not limited to—gender inequality, amid the mythos surrounding gender norms and stereotypes. The Montgomery family motto is "Guarde Bien." The family crest depicts a woman balancing an anchor in one hand and a man's decapitated head in the other. True to my ancestry, I will cut down anything that would silence the voice I've fought so hard to cultivate and own, and the voices of others in the progressive high-vibrational collective. For the record, Montgomery was my mother's maiden name, and is my adopted matrilineal maiden name, hence, my daughter's maiden name, a powerful nod to the matriarchal construct I unknowingly created through a legal name change on my 18th birthday.

My road hasn't been easy. Society groomed me to feel guilt and shame over gender-based crimes committed against my person. I was told to speak in hushed whispers, eyes cast down, hands folded neatly in my lap, with ankles crossed demurely. The unspoken agreement in our patriarchal society is, no matter how many times one of the "weaker" sex is beaten, molested, or raped, they should remain passive, submissive, and non-confrontational. This is the standard for feminine behavior set by society's anachronistic norms, evidenced by the plethora of hush money trials, coercion, and threats made by political leaders in order to silence women. When women do speak out, as so many did during "Me Too," they're questioned regarding their actions and attire and if they had, in fact, placed themselves in a position to be assaulted. This blame-shifting is the biggest hypocrisy that we women are taught. From an early age we learn to embrace this idea of femininity, and also accept the default judgment that, in doing so, we are the architects of any misfortune that we may experience.

I was born into the era of the Civil Rights Movement, I witnessed Roe v. Wade, then women burning their bras, but I often say I wasn't born—I was forged. I've survived just about every type of patriarchal abuse from birth onward, beginning with father estrangement/stepfather physical abuse, childhood clergy abuse and kidnapping/sex trafficking, which culminated in adult relationships with narcissists that found me "picking the father wound." From an early age I was indoctrinated into the hierarchy of God atop the Holy Trinity, below that old white men and their wives—who miraculously spawned from their rib, and then everyone else, depending on skin color, educational/financial status, and political beliefs. The first rule of the patriarchy is: God created woman for man. He created lesser humans to subjugate themselves to elitist rulers, animals for human consumption, and the Earth for the white man to conquer. "Girls" could join a profession, preferably as nurses or teachers, but, no matter the path, they were wives and mothers first, and Barbie's body was the body of choice.

As a child in the '70s, I caught my first glimpse of the battle between the sexes. One of my first Barbies was Adolescent Skipper. When one rotated her arm a full 360-degree revolution, her tits grew. Conversely, my big brother's GI Joe had no such messaging. GI Joe's charge was to remain stoic at all times. I only learned later in life that we each have, within us, both feminine and masculine energy. However, I was groomed to believe there was something wrong with me if I had empathy, yet a warrior's spirit.

I grew up within a society that historically encouraged men to embrace the masculine, and women the feminine. I just spent a few days, half-naked in the desert, pondering gender issues and rape culture in the Information Age, where I was reminded that it wasn't always this way. Many Native American tribes recognized five genders, and women and matriarchs were held in high esteem. Sexual violence did not appear to be standard, and was punished in tribal adjudication. This lack of gender violence was even more pronounced in Mesoamerica, ruled by the Aztecan goddesses until Hernán Cortés and his white male God invaded, wielding a shield of religious righteousness, which hid an imperialistic genocidal agenda. Fast forward to 2025, where a sense of schadenfreude exists between two very divisive political parties, but more specifically between a bastardized version of Christianity co-opted by the Republican Party and those who recognize the danger that these beliefs pose: A potential imposition of a sharia-law like state, in which misogyny is no longer hidden, but becomes the law of the land. Hints of this dystopian future are evidenced by the recent reversal of Roe v. Wade and the denigration of leftist women, LGBTQ, and anyone else who doesn't vote Red.

Misogyny, though pervasive in politics and religious dogma, exists because society still perceives men as more powerful than women. Without deconstructing these patriarchal structures there is no path forward. Most men are taught from childhood that being vulnerable and in touch with their "feminine energy" is somehow emasculating, and that women can't be both feminine and masculine, expressing both "feminine energy" and the so-called "masculine energy" traits society still vilifies and fears when expressed by women. Inversely, women are taught that men are wired to hunt and spread their seed, which basically green-lights predation. Balance can only be restored through recognizing and acknowledging both toxic masculinity and femininity, and understanding and correcting the unhealthy mindset paradigm, thus freeing both men and women from the constraints of gender-normative oppression. In this new world, women would step into their new skin and embrace their hard-fought and well-deserved wisdom and power.

Resistance Online
By Marissa DeAngelis

Online we are driving ourselves crazy, giving attention to negative entities, the worst people, and the politicians that are doing us harm. Here's what we need to do instead:

Be Your Own Gate-Keeper.

Protect yourself, like a bouncer at the front door of a club, from the crazy party that is social media. Decide what to give your attention to. Billionaires are fighting more for your attention than your money. It's the scrolling. We're all addicted to it. Delete one or two of the apps that are stealing your attention. Use timers that alert you to your time spent on each app. Observe how long you spend on each site, and at what time of day you scroll, and assign yourself rules. See how much time you're spending on social media and then cut it down. Doom-scrolling, as they call it, is not making us better or changing anything.

Learn Differently

Find one or two causes that you're passionate about and learn about them the old-fashioned way, with books, and the not old-fashioned way, with podcasts. Find out what laws are being passed around the country, rather than what the pundits are saying on television. What people say and what people do are two very different things. Know the difference.

Listen to Others

TikTok may not be long in this country, but if it is, I recommend investigating TikTok Lives, where people of all kinds talk about issues. Be aware that it runs the gamut from extremely smart people and extremely not-so-smart people who say shockingly stupid things. But I have learned more about what the public is thinking on TikTok than anywhere else. For example, when everyone else was shocked that IVF clinics were being closed down in some states I was not, because I had been listening to pro-lifers talk for over a year about how unethical they were. As a pro-choice woman it was shocking to hear, but I sat back and listened. And I found ways to look for the middle-ground on many issues, because often many people are just looking for a polite conversation.

I also keyed in on specific language being used within the pro-life movement that wasn't being used 20 years ago, That language is now being used to flip young people into either not caring about abortion rights, or it is used to sway them into positions that they didn't have before. Studying these tactics is good prep for swaying people back to your own side, on any issue. People on the Right are organized, and they train people on another app called Discord to argue against every pro-choice argument. They are relentless, no matter how ridiculous they sound.

If you are passionate about climate change or immigration laws or abortion rights, TikTok Lives is a good place to listen to what the other side is doing and to do actual reconnaissance work.

Educate Others

Talk to people around you about fact checking, and show them how you do it. I tell people that I have a journalism background, and that when I've researched something it means that I didn't pull it from a CNN or Fox News article. It means I Googled the phrase "fact check" with the appropriate word or question, and then read multiple fact-checking sites like politifact.org, Snopes, and factcheck, org, in order to get entire histories of the accusation at hand. I also look at statistics and data from more than one source (CDC, Statista, etc.). I compare sources like Pew Research against some of these to see the disparities, but I make sure the essence of what they're showing is the same. Very often people are using clips of podcasts as sources, which, I have to say, drives me bananas.

Know When to Go

Have certain exit strategies ready to go when you find yourself talking to an idiot. I stopped long ago engaging too far with people who say, "Everyone has their own opinion" or "Well, I heard that…" I have actually stopped a few people who are in mid-sentence and said, "I have to step away from this because I'm smarter and more informed than you on this topic." That may not be the ideal approach, but there are objective facts, I know there is a knowledge gap, and a lot of people cling to conspiracy theories because they're easier to understand. It's an issue all over the world, but it's really bad in this country.

Sometimes, I actually throw in a Donald Trump compliment and say, "One thing I learned from Donald Trump is to point when someone is a low-intellect person, so I don't sugarcoat things anymore." Sometimes I tell them, "This conversation is beneath me." Keep in mind, though, this is when people have come at me with stuff like "Everyone who comes from the southern border is Mexican and not from any other countries." Or, "Covid isn't real because it can't be detected with a blood test." Or they don't know the branches of government. Either way, know when you have to duck out.

Keep safe out there. And resist.

Marissa DeAngelis is the author of *The Binge Watcher's Guide to The Golden Girls* and contributed to *Miss Pamela's Writing School for Electric Ladies.* She holds a BA in journalism from the University of Maryland with a minor in film and comparative literature. She lived and worked in New York City as a copywriter for over a decade and moved to Los Angeles in 2020 to continue her writing pursuits. While living in New York, she performed standup comedy and would like to start that up again in California. She considers herself a cinephile and would love to write a fictionalized novel about old Hollywood one day.

Resistance and Me
By Ed Stein

Ed Stein was the editorial cartoonist for the (Denver) Rocky Mountain News for 31 years. My work was syndicated by United Features and Universal Press to more than 400 dailies.

Resistance is My Favorite Baseball Cap
By David Freed

Many folks have a favorite ballcap. This one, with its sweat stains and frayed brim, happens to be mine. In all the time I've worn it, however, I can recall only one person ever making mention of the blue and gold-winged panther sewn on its crown.

We were at a restaurant a couple of years back in Colorado Springs. The receptionist, an African American woman in her early 20's, was guiding us to our table. "I like your hat," she said, smiling at me over her shoulder. "The Fighting 99th."

That anyone, especially one so young, would recognize the unit patch worn by fighter pilots of the 99th Pursuit Squadron, the famed, all-Black Tuskegee Airmen who flew against Hitler's Luftwaffe in World War II, left me a little stunned. I asked her how she knew about them

"My great-grandfather," she said, "was a Tuskegee airman." I will never forget the pride in her eyes as she told me.

Anyone who has ever studied American military history knows the inspirational story of the Tuskegee Airmen. Treated as second-class citizens because of the color of their skin, they overcame every obstacle imaginable, first learning to fly in rural, racist Alabama, before distinguishing themselves in the hostile skies over Europe. Along the way, they became known as the "Red Tails" by virtue of the distinctive color with which they adorned the empennages of their P-47 Thunderbolts and P-51 Mustangs. So fabled were their achievements in combat that more than 70 years later, in 2018, when U.S. Air Force commanders were debating what name to assign their new primary jet trainer, the Boeing-Saab T-7, they chose the "Red Hawk" and ordered the jets' tails painted red to honor those Tuskegee warriors.

As a pilot, I've always dreamed of flying a Mustang. I never have. I've never even sat in one. I was born long after the end of World War II and, for the record, I'm not Black. So you might be asking, what business does a guy like me have wearing a ball cap sporting a Tuskegee squadron patch? The simple answer is this: Every time I do, I am reminded of the debt of gratitude we owe to those men, and to the millions of others of every ethnicity who fought and sometimes died to leave our world a better, fairer, more equal place.

Which brings me to Donald Trump.

To comply with his crackdown on diversity, equality, and inclusion initiatives, the Air Force decided to remove all videos of the Tuskegee Airmen from its basic training courses. Also scrapped were videos featuring the WASPs, the Women Airforce Service Pilots who played a vital role ferrying military aircraft during the war. Almost immediately, Pete Hegseth, Trump's preposterously unqualified Secretary of Defense and a former Fox News talking head, bowed to broad outrage, reversed course, and announced that the videos would be reinstated—a rare act of morality in an Administration that prides itself on immorality, exclusion, and outright cruelty at virtually every turn.

While I can't conceive what cultural harm could possibly come from teaching new Air Force recruits about the courage and sacrifices of such extraordinary heroes, I can easily envision the dangers posed in redrafting history, as Trump and his minions appear to be trying on every front.

To marginalize or exclude the contributions made to the common good by any group is to erase their presence in the shared story of our nation. By failing to acknowledge the unique achievements and sacrifices made by heroes who first had to overcome scorn and hate from their own countrymen, we risk not only distorting the past but also spitting on the very values that made America great—perseverance and unity in the face of unimaginable adversity. By deleting the stories of trailblazers like the Tuskegee Airmen and the WASPs, we also deny future generations of vital role models—the very individuals who represent the best of what we as a people have always strived to be.

The legacy left by these pioneers—who fought both on the front lines and against the prejudices of their own country—is not merely a story of military valor; it is a testament to the strength of the human spirit, and to the conviction that ability is not defined by the color of one's skin or gender, but indeed by the content of one's character. None of those pioneers served to gain celebrity or riches. They did so because they believed in the promise of a better, more just America. To blot out their stories as if they never existed is to ignore their influence in whatever progress we've made toward achieving the kind of America for which they fought so hard.

And, so, until it falls off my head from use, I will continue wearing my well-loved cap with its squadron patch honoring the pilots of the Fighting 99th, both as a testament to their bravery and as my responsibility to help ensure in my small way that their story is not forgotten. Whether in the skies or on the ground, the Tuskegee Airmen and all those who served alongside them strived to pave the way for a future in which every American would have the opportunity to soar. We owe it to them—and to ourselves—to keep their stories alive, to remind the world that "Make America Great" is more than a political slogan. It is courage; it is self-sacrifice; it is devotion to a transcendent ideal, as yet unrealized, of that shining city on the hill.

David Fred is the author of the best-selling Cordell Logan mystery series. Freed is an instrument-rated pilot and a former investigative reporter for the *Los Angeles Times*, where he shared in a Pulitzer Prize for coverage of the Rodney King riots.

I Testify

By Jess Piper

The world is on fire and none of us can do much to stop it on our own, but we can each do a little to stop it, and those actions add up to a massive resistance.

Red state residents recognize the shock and awe doctrine that we are all seeing from the first few days of the Trump administration. It's something we have a lot of experience working with. Our nervous systems are already familiar with the constant attacks on democracy—the constant need to keep up with what our lawmakers are doing and pushback when necessary.

I live in Missouri. I have lived under the tyranny of a GOP supermajority for two decades. It's not easy, but I have learned to make calls and post and write and then get outside. Do the work and then take a break.

My emboldened lawmakers do whatever they want. They will not honor the will of the people, so they need constant pushback from the people. We have been fighting in this way for over two decades.

The only way to stop them is through constant resistance. Because screw them and their authoritarian instincts! We didn't elect kings, and I won't have a boot on my neck, and I won't stand for one on my neighbor's neck.

We can't be shocked into silence.

Yesterday, I drove to the Missouri Capitol to testify against something that has already been resolved: Abortion.

Here is my testimony to the committee at the Missouri Capitol. This was my act of defiance and resistance:

My testimony against SJR 54, Jefferson City, MO. 2/4/25.

Hello. My name is Jess Piper and I am here to testify against HJR 54. This resolution is an attempt to overturn the will of Missouri voters.

The Republicans who are behind this fake resolution claim to represent rural people. They don't and I am here to set that record straight.

I am a rural mom to five and grandmother to four. I live in Northwest Missouri and I am angry about the overreach of the Missouri GOP. I am here to testify on the disrespect—the absolute disdain—shown to every Missouri voter by some of the folks in this room.

Amendment 3 passed in Missouri. There is no reason why I had to drive eight hours round trip to testify against an abortion restriction. Why can't you just accept the will of your constituents?

I collected signatures for Amendment 3 in some of the most rural areas of this state. Brookfield is a town of 4,000 and when I pulled up to set up my table and gather signatures, there were folks in the parking lot waiting. A woman signed her name and then texted her Bible group to remind them to come sign the amendment.

Ever heard of Marceline? The town has a population of 2,000. A woman I met in Marceline who chored her animals and farm—and then came to sign the amendment in overalls and mucks. She knew what she was signing, and I am here to give her voice. It's hard to get your chores done and make it all the way to Jeff City to testify against legislation and your own lawmakers who won't honor your vote or your voice.

I bet many of you know where Maryville is. We were able to get a few hundred signatures in that town. Maryville is a "huge urban space" in the middle of cornfields, population 11k. They even have a Starbucks. I sat at that coffee shop for hours one afternoon to get signatures. When I was about to pack up, a man named Gordon came in to add his name to the petition.

Gordon is 86 years old. He uses a walker and drove all the way to town and proudly signed his name to a petition to make sure his great-granddaughters would not suffer under the tyranny of an abortion ban.

I am here to remind you that lawmakers who would overturn the will of Missourians should remember they serve the folks who sent them here, and many of those folks voted to approve abortion rights in this state.

Those people include the Bible group from Brookfield and the farmer from Marceline and the great-grandfather from Maryville.

I am also here to express my disgust with the Missouri GOP. You claim to be the party of "small government" but that is a lie. You want to control books, curriculum, teachers, children's private parts, and every uterus in the state. You overreach into the lives of Missouri citizens each day.

You can't be the party of "small government" when your members act like tyrants. Do better.

It's as easy as that.

Well, it wasn't that easy—I had to drive all day to speak for three minutes, but it was worth every mile. They were forced to listen to someone they have tried to disenfranchise. They were forced to see my face and listen to my scathing review of their tenure. They couldn't escape me or the dozens who testified against the resolution to ban abortion... again.

I know how hard every day is, but do one thing today.

Share an article with friends and then call your Congressional Rep to demand they hold the line with Musk. Call your Senators and demand they do the same. Call you AG and demand they stand with the American people on the biggest data breach in American history—sue Elon for stealing the data of the people of their State.

And then go outside if you can.

Don't be paralyzed in front of the television or your phone. Doom-scrolling without action will make you crazy and exhaust you. That's the point of shock and awe.

Do one thing. And then rest.

Rinse. Repeat.

P.S. I am so thankful for the Abortion Action group and the Missouri ACLU who planned the resistance event at the Capitol. There were so many Missourians there to oppose SJR 54 that we filled the hearing room and an overflow room. The hearing went on for several hours with testimony opposing the resolution.

This is what democracy looks like.

This essay appeared on Jess Piper's Substack account in February, 2025, The View from Rural Missouri.

Jess Piper is the Executive Director of Blue Missouri. She is a grassroots organizer, writer, and educator. Former State House nominee. Rural mom fighting for rural schools.

The Handmaid's Tale is Now
By Sherri Donovan

(This essay was written in 2022, but is
unfortunately very relevant today)

I remember meeting Supreme Court Justice Brennan in his chambers at the Supreme Court when I was in law school. With his eyes sparkling brightly, he told me that it was letters from women around the country that inspired his vote and determination for Roe v. Wade. My late term abortion was traumatic enough when a hole in the stomach of the fetus was discovered. I cannot imagine if I would have been forced to carry to full term only to give birth to a dead fetus. I am forever grateful to a Planned Parenthood clinic in Vermont that assisted me with an early abortion. My friend Donna had an ectopic pregnancy and would have been dead if not for her abortion. My mother was forced to do a dangerous back alley abortion in Puerto Rico because abortion was not legal. My daughter is distraught that she and possible children in the future will have fewer rights than her mother and their grandmother.

Dobbs v. Jackson Women's Health Organization will go down in history and herstory as a catastrophic Supreme Court decision. I was appalled that Alito, who writes for the majority compares overturning Plessy v. Ferguson which legalized race segregation to the Dobbs decision which overturns Roe v. Wade and permits the restriction of a women's rights to control her own body.

The Dobbs majority completely ignores the Women's rights movement and advances over the last century and recent decades. It completely ignores that it is a matter of healthcare, life, liberty and privacy for women. The majority opinion refuses to recognize that the clear majority of the US population is in favor of pro-choice. More than two-thirds of Americans are in favor of retaining Roe. One quarter of American women will have an abortion before the age of 45.

The Supreme Court does not mention that this decision is out of step with the rest of the world. Over the past several decades, more than 50 countries throughout Asia, Africa, Europe and the Americas have liberalized their abortion laws. Latin American countries have more reproductive rights than the women in the USA. Only the United States, Poland and Nicaragua have reduced abortion access in the 21st century. Canada has decriminalized abortion at any point in a pregnancy. Most Western European countries impose restrictions on abortion after 12 to 14 weeks, but they often have liberal exceptions to those time limits, including to prevent harm to a woman's physical or mental health.

The Court without unanimous support overturns precedent of two Supreme Court decisions, Roe v. Wade, and Casey v. Planned Parenthood and more than 20 other cases reaffirming or applying the constitutional right to abortion. There is no change in law or fact that necessitated this drastic, action. As the dissent in Dobbs makes clear, "Casey is a precedent about precedent. It reviewed the same arguments made here in support of overruling Roe, and it found that doing so was not warranted."

The Alito decision is stuck in the criminal earlier history of abortion. Women were chattel in this country and could not own property, vote or obtain a credit card or law license. How far back would these extreme right judges and appointees of Trump go? The dissent points out that, "The majority makes this change based on the question: Did the reproductive right recognized in Roe and Casey exist in "1868, the year when the Fourteenth Amendment was Ratified? ...Those responsible for the original Cons-titution, including the Fourteenth Amendment, did not perceive women as equals, and did not recognize women's rights. When the majority says that we must read our foundational charter as viewed at the time of ratification (except that we may also check it against the Dark Ages), it consigns women to second class citizenship." The dissent continues, "...our point is different: It is that applications of liberty and equality can evolve while remaining grounded in constitutional principles, constitutional history, and constitutional precedents. Roe and Casey fit neatly into a long line of decisions protecting from government intrusion a wealth of private choices about family matters, child rearing, intimate relationships, and procreation... In the Fourteenth Amendment's terms, it takes away her [a woman's] liberty. In conclusion, Kagan, Sotomayor and Breyer state "With sorrow — for this Court, but more, for the many millions of American women who have today lost a fundamental constitutional protection — we dissent."

According to the majority of the US Supreme Court, guns have more rights than women over their bodies. The hypocrisy and blatant political nature of the Dobbs decision is clear. In their opinion June 23, 2022 forcing New York and other densely populated states to allow more handguns in public and causing more danger to the public, the conservative majority, led by Justice Clarence Thomas, argued that medieval law imposing arms restrictions —specifically, the 1328 Statute of Northampton —"has little bearing on the Second Amendment" because it was "enacted... more than 450 years before the ratification of the Constitution." Yet in their ruling the next day, June 24, 2022 in Dobbs v. Jackson Women's Health, setting women's rights back half a century the conservative justices, led by Samuel Alito (who was also in the guns majority) and joined by Thomas, argued precisely the opposite. They justified abortion bans by citing, among others, "Henry de Bracton's 13th-century treatise." That was written circa 1250 and referred to monsters, duels, burning at the stake —and to women as property, "inferior" to men. The moral hypocrisy about helping families and children is noted when considering that, a state-by-state analysis by public health professionals shows that States with the most restrictive abortion policies also continue to invest the least in women's and children's health, as the Dobbs dissent exemplifies.

The dissent begins by stating, "For half a century, Roe v. Wade, 410 U. S. 113 (1973), and Planned Parenthood of Southeastern Pa. v. Casey, 505 U. S. 833 (1992), have protected the liberty and equality of women. Respecting a woman as an autonomous being, and granting her full equality, meant giving her substantial choice over this most personal and most consequential of all life decisions... Today's Court, that is, does not think there is anything of constitutional significance attached to a woman's control of her body and the path of her life". The dissenting opinion written jointly by Justices Sonia Sotomayor, Elana Kagan and Stephen Breyer states that the Court is "rescinding an individual right in its entirety and conferring it on the State, an action the Court takes for the first time in history." The Dobbs dissent points out that the majority's brazen rejection of stare decisis, respect for precedent, "breaches a core rule-of-law principle, designed to promote constancy in the law." The dissent said the majority's refusal to address real world consequences "reveals how little it knows or cares about women's lives or about the suffering its decision will cause." The dissent raised questions about rape, incest, threats to a mother's life, interstate travel for abortion, morning-after pills, IUDs, and in vitro fertilization. The dissent writes, "Most threatening of all, no language in today's decision stops the Federal Government from prohibiting abortions nationwide, once again from the moment of conception and without exceptions for rape or incest. If that happens, "the views of [an individual State's] citizens" will not matter… The majority's refusal even to consider the life-altering consequences of reversing Roe and Casey is a stunning indictment,"

Even Chief Justice Roberts admonished fellow conservatives for cavalierly overturning the Roe v. Wade super-precedent. "Surely we should adhere closely to principles of judicial restraint here, where the broader path the court chooses entails repudiating a constitutional right we have not only previously recognized, but also expressly reaffirmed" Roberts wrote, The majority's "dramatic and consequential ruling is unnecessary," and "a serious jolt to the legal system".

The concurrence of Clarence Thomas makes specific reference to overturning other well established precedents that rely on the 14th Amendment. He cites Griswald which concerns the right to use birth control; Lawrence v. Texas protecting consensual adult sex and Obergefell granting the right to same sex marriage. How peculiar he does not mention Loving v Virginia which relies on the same constitutional principles and protects interracial marriage. Justice Clarence Thomas's separate concurrence made crystal clear that he would indeed do away with the entire substantive due-process doctrine on which the right to abortion rested. As the Justices Sotomayor, Kagan & Breyer sharply note in the dissent, "Either the mass of the majority's opinion is hypocrisy, or additional constitutional rights are under threat. It is one or the other."

Pregnant women, health care providers, pharmacists, as well as possibly volunteers, family members, friends and anyone who has significant contact may be investigated, or arrested as suspect if a pregnancy does not end as a healthy birth. Surveillance will certainly increase. Half the States will move to outlaw or restrict abortion. Will there be trials and investigations if a miscarriage is murder? In certain States, Women now risk criminal prosecution for ordering a day after pill. Health care providers will now have the dilemma of letting women die or suffer serious injury or risk loss of their license or a lawsuit if they perform an abortion. Poor, Black & women of color will be punished the most. Approximately 52% of women of childbearing age will face abortion restrictions. During the past four years, 11 states have passed abortion bans that contain no exceptions for rape or incest. In Texas, already, children aged nine, 10, and 11, who don't yet understand what sex and abuse are, face forced pregnancy and childbirth after being raped. States might also ban other reproductive practices, such as in vitro fertilization or the use of intrauterine devices.

What is to be done?

1. Utilize your First Amendment right to protest.
2. Join and support reproductive rights organizations and organizations assisting women in States that restrict abortion and other reproductive rights/ birth control options.
3. Support electoral candidates that advocate for abortion rights.
4. Get active in the mid-term elections.
5. Advocate for the passage of federal legislation to codify Roe.
6. Advocate for the immediate addition of judges to the Supreme Court and other judicial reforms.
7. Learn and teach women how to protect their privacy to avoid unintentionally providing possible evidence to prosecutors who can get access to information through health care institutions and technological devices.
8. Utilize and share the following resources: If you need to find a clinic or help people find a clinic: https://www.ineedana.com/ • Text 'hello' to 202-883-4620 Abortion Funds in Every State: https://donations4abortion.com/ • Twitter: @helmsinki created this website/resource of abortion funds Keep our clinics — https://keepourclinics.org/ •Independent clinics provide 2/3 of abortions in the US. • Twitter: @AbortionCare All Options: https://all-options.networkforgood.com/ • Provides pregnancy options counseling and financial support for abortion seekers. Practical support groups: https://www.apiarycollective.org/our-work •Brigid: https://brigidalliance.org/donation/ • MAC: https://midwestaccesscoalition.org/pages/donate • Digital defense fund: https://digitaldefensefund.org/ • Reproductive Health App Euki (created with privacy in mind): https://eukiapp.com/ Reproductive • Legal Defense Fund https://reprolegaldefensefund.org/ • Twitter: @reprolegalfund Reproductive Legal Help Line: http://www.reprolega lhelpline.org/ •Call 844-868-2812 •Message

through online secure form IWRising: https://iwrising.org • Financial and practical support for Indigenous abortion seekers •Twitter: @IWRising Self-Managed Abortion information: https://reprocare.com • Twitter: @reprocarefund • Can call or text at 1-833-226-7821 for information, support, and referrals. For adolescents and minors under 18 who need an abortion: https://janesdueprocess.org/ • Twitter @JanesDueProcess • Can call or text at 866-999-5263 and they will help them navigate the process. 722 West 168th Street, New York, NY 10032 Telephone: 212.342.5127 Abortion Squad combats abortion-related misinformation: https://onlineabortionresources.org • Twitter @Abortion_Squad •Funding for their work: https://ko-fi.com/abortion squadSupport and follow the leadership of Reproductive Justice Organizations (here are a handful): SisterSong: https://www.sisters ong.net/reproductive-justice •Black Mamas Matter Alliance: https://blackmamasmatter.org/ • In our own voice — National Black Women's Reproductive Justice Agenda: https://blackrj.org/ • SisterLove: https://www.sisterlove.org • Spark Reproductive Justice Now!: http://www.sparkrj.org Rebecca Gomperts, who leads Aid Access, an organization based in Austria is openly providing abortion pills to women in prohibition states, and has been safely mailing abortion pills to pregnant people all over the world since 2005, with the organization Women on Web.

Sherri Donovan is a family mediator, neutral evaluator, collaborative practitioner and parent coordinator. She was also an adjunct professor of forensic psychology and family law at the Derner Institute of Advanced Psychological Studies, Adelphi University. As director of the Sherri Donovan & Associates, P.C. Family Center in New York City, and a practice for nearly 30 years, Sherri has assisted over 8000 families. She has lectured extensively on family dispute resolution for the United Nations, AFCC, Academy of Professional Family Mediators, Association of Divorce Financial Planners, and the Forensic and Family Law Training Program. Sherri is also the President of Art Helping Life, Inc., a nonprofit that is currently conducting educational programs for children in West Africa and providing material support.

Sherri is a published author and blogger. *Reflections* is her second book of poetry. Her first poetry book is entitled, *Matryoshka Rising*. Her poems have also been published in the Poetry Anthology. Sherri has also performed her poems at the Cornelia Street Cafe, New York County Lawyers Association, and in-salon poetry circles internationally.

Her articles have appeared in *The Huffington Post, New York Law Journal, Cosmopolitan* and *Parent Magazine*, as well as in the collections of essays, *#MeToo: Essays About How and Why This Happened, What It Means and How to Make Sure It Never Happens Again*

Sherri Donovan is the founder of the nonprofit, Art Helping Life, Inc. and has traveled to 136 countries. After many years in New York City, Sherri is currently residing in Oyster Bay, Long Island. You can read more blog posts from Sherri Donovan at Sherridonovan.com/Sherri's blog.

Breathing Through Pain
By Brittney Nickerson

Some days I feel a pain that rivals anything I have ever felt before. My chronic inflammation seizes my low back and right hip, making me clutch a heating pad like a lifeline. I lay immobile on my bed, the couch, the floor. My chest rises and falls, as I force myself to breathe. Eventually, the pain will become bearable again. It always does.

I was working long days in education, supporting teachers and children learning science. I wanted to make a difference in the world—I still do. Some days I know I made people's lives better but mine was not. There were many times when I spoke as the lone voice in a room, asking not to take advantage of teachers' time, to pay them more, to actually listen to them, to not take for granted the fact that so many of them are used to working long, thankless days.

My pain began pushing its way to the top of my mind. I could not think about the teachers or the children. I could not think about how I was not doing enough, as I was working on weekends and holidays. As I began to face backlash for speaking up.

I dragged myself to my bed and laid there, trying to breathe.

It has always been dangerous for me to lay still. Thoughts sneak into my brain, pulling at my doubt and siphoning my self-esteem. Where is my productivity? My purpose? What am I other than a pile of potential, wasting away under the constant re-emergence of my chronic pain?

How can I do anything meaningful, when some days, I can't even sit in a chair?

Like many others, I struggled to develop a community after COVID. One of the ways I tried to remedy that was volunteering for a nonprofit. One summer, I participated in a workshop. For some reason, I was embarrassed to be there. Maybe it was because I was the only one still wearing a mask, or perhaps it was because I left early to help manage my pain.

As I sat there, words from the facilitator pierced through my insecurity and aching. "Self-advocacy," she said, "is a form of leadership."

I left my job. There was no progress, only pain and a suffocating sense of dread that made it hard to breathe. When I walked out the door for the last time, I felt powerful. My life was under my control. I finally had the time and resources to pursue a diagnosis for my chronic pain. It has since gotten better, but some days, it still makes me lightheaded and nauseous. Some days, I'm still finding comfort in a heating pad and the carpet of my floor.

I started reaching out to more people. We would go on walks together, and they would patiently wait for me when I needed to take a break. We spoke to each other in our stillness. They sought to understand my pain, and I sought to understand theirs.

Less than a year ago, I was broke. The world felt like it was falling apart and I did too. I sat on the phone for hours, talking with my friends, my family, and my peers. We spoke of our fears and our desperation. We shared our stories: How I began to walk again, and how they did too.

Today, we are continually faced with change. As people flock to the streets in protest over the new administration, I remember the versatility of resistance. I remember the cost of walking, of breathing, of getting up off the floor.

The rapid enactment of Trump's executive orders is designed to cause dysfunction. The intent is to terrify us into relinquishing our power, to overwhelm us into believing there is nothing we can do.

But that's not true.

Resistance is in my ability to work productively remotely, it's in the contract I draft to protect my writing from being fed to generative AI, it's in the anxiety-ridden phone calls where I negotiate a fair salary, and it's in the problem solving I do with my friend who does not know how they will repay their student loans. Resistance is in my ability to advocate for myself and to support my community to do the same. Resistance is in my commitment to listen to other people's stories and to share my own, so that when the pain gets overwhelming, we can hold onto each other like heating pads, and breathe through it together.

Brittney Nickerson is the author of the short story "Lost Shoes," as well as the creator of all content on the blog *Sojourner Soul*. She was born and raised in a small town deep in the woods of Maine with the remnants of a junkyard in her family's backyard. Years of digging glass coke bottles out of the dirt inspired her down a path of archaeology, anthropology, and ethnographic research. Her studies enable her deep curiosity and love for understanding the human experience, which she channels into her writing.

She continues to live in Maine, and when she is not exploring new stories, she is often found exploring the wilderness.

The Importance of Mindful Communication

By James Martorano

One glaring aspect of our times that separates it from all others is the incessant flow of information. Whether through emails, texts, social media posts, television commentaries, politicians' assertions, press conferences, or even face-to-face communications, we are exposed to a relentless bombardment of statements asserted as facts. Putting aside our arduous task of distinguishing truth from lies, fact from fiction, I pose a more preliminary question: what should the communicator consider before making their assertion in the first place?

To find an answer I started my research by scouring my papers from my graduate school philosophy classes. To my delight, I came across my notes on Buddhism. Although I don't subscribe to everything, I found Buddha's teachings on mindful communication to be totally on point.

Buddha suggests five key considerations before you send that email, issue that tweet, publish that post, state your opinion, or make that statement at a press conference:

1) Is it true?

It seems elementary, my dear Watson, but in this day and age of misinformation, disinformation, and outright lying, it is important to check and cross-check your sources to make sure that what you are claiming to be a fact is exactly that. Buddha's teachings encourage us to ensure that what we state or write is accurate and reflective of reality, not some rumor, conspiracy nonsense, or partisan slant.

Why is this important? The rise of fake news, misinformation, disinformation and conspiracy theories makes it essential to pursue truth in all our communications. By adhering to Buddha's first and most important consideration-truth-we can foster a culture of honesty that combats the rampant spread of falsehoods. Engaging in thoughtful conversations, fact checking, and being open to different perspectives can help create a more informed society. This commitment to truth fosters trust and accountability in our relationships and communities.

2) Is it necessary?

Not all truths need to be spoken. Evaluating whether something needs to be said helps us avoid unnecessary conflict or pain. In many situations, silence can be more powerful than words.

Why should we consider this? The world feels more polarized than ever, with differing opinions often leading to hostility. Emphasizing this second consideration-necessity-can help individuals think before they speak, potentially diffusing tensions before they escalate. By focusing on what truly needs to be said we can avoid unnecessary arguments and promote understanding. By considering the necessity of our speech we can promote peace rather than discord, a crucial aspect in today's often divisive climate.

3) Is it kind?

Although I sound like an old fogey here, kindness, in my judgment, is a desperately needed virtue in this era of take-no-prisoners, mean-spirited communication. Buddha asserted that kindness is the cornerstone of compassionate communication. Before speaking, we should reflect on whether our words are offered with love and understanding. I know this sounds alien in today's world, but I wholeheartedly believe that choosing kindness can be revolutionary. It builds connections and promotes healing. Social media platforms often amplify negativity, making it easy to forget this important value. By prioritizing kindness in our speech, we can counteract the harshness prevalent in online interactions. Small acts of kindness, such as offering compliments or expressing appreciation, can ripple outwards, inspiring others to do the same. I am not naïve; I don't expect to hear kind words flowing from the mouths or pens of those who have found success stoking hate. But that doesn't mean we have to follow suit.

4) Is it helpful?

Words have the power to uplift or undermine. It is vital to assess the potential impact of our statements. Sharing information or opinions that genuinely help others strengthens community bonds and enhances collective well-being. In contrast, careless or derogatory words can lead to further distress, especially when people are already grappling with their struggles. Why does this matter? Given the complexities of today's social issues, ensuring our words are helpful becomes imperative. This means engaging in discussions that are solution-oriented and constructive rather than merely critical. By sharing insights and offering support, we contribute to dialogue that helps communities move forward. Sadly, too often, I find statements made by people in the public eye to be consistently unhelpful, destructive, and undermining of goodwill.

5) Is it timely?

Context matters. Our words should not only be true, necessary, kind, and helpful, but also timely. Timing can enhance the effectiveness of communication. Speaking out of turn or when emotions are heightened can lead to misunderstanding and conflict. Recognizing the right moment to share thoughts is crucial for constructive dialogue.

The digital age has blurred the line between personal interaction and public discourse, often leading to hasty reactions. Recognizing the importance of timing allows us to choose when to engage thoughtfully, preserving the integrity of our message. This awareness can prevent miscommunication and encourage deeper understanding.

Our age is completely alien from the one that existed when Buddha walked the earth. Yet his insights are as relevant and insightful today as they were during his time. His guidance transcends time and cultural boundaries. In a world that can often feel harsh and unkind, these principles serve as a beacon, reminding us of the power of our words and writings, and the responsibility we shoulder in our communications. Embracing truth, necessity, kindness, helpfulness, and timeliness enhances not only our relationships, but also contributes positively to society at large.

In all my years in public office, I sought to follow these principles in my words and actions. The truth mattered to me and still does. I never once spoke with malice or hate, always trying to emphasize the positive, as I traversed a partisan battlefield.

My friends, it's up to all of us. We can do better.

James Martorano has written approximately 800 essays published over a 14 year period (2011-present). The essays have explored a wide range of topics such as Quantum computers, the Meaning of Life, Albert Einstein's brain crossing the county in the trunk of a Buick, A letter to my great-great-granddaughter, who I will never meet, Japanese Cinema, the need for critical thinking in an age of irrationality, etc.

He holds a Masters in philosophy and a JD from Fordham Law, and has taught philosophy. In his former job as an attorney for the Legal Aid Society in the Bronx (45 years) he had the honor of training hundreds of attorneys on trial practice. He is presently still writing and still practicing law in his own practice in New York.

Miniature, Ubiquitous, and Deadly:
Fractal Resistance to the Tiniest Microcosm of Tyranny
By Jill Nagle

When I tell people that I am writing a book about the one two-letter word in the English language that hijacks our minds, and how to reclaim clarity, connection, freedom, and joy, I often ask them to guess what the word is. They usually answer,

"*No?*"

"Wrong, but that's the most common guess."

"Hmm. *Me?*"

"That's the second most common guess, also wrong. You're in good company—almost no one guesses what the word is. However I just said it, and have said it a couple of times already.

Pause.

"Uhhhhh... *it?*"

"Nope."

By this point they're mystified, and perhaps a bit frustrated. And I'm marveling again at how such a powerful world can remain hidden in plain sight from... well, almost everyone I've talked to.

So finally I tell them,

"The word is... *is.*"

They stare blankly.

I elaborate, but not as much as I'm about to do right now.

When we talk about what "is," we *externally reference*, or *outsource reality*, to an authority that may or may not exist. This works just fine when we have a common source of truth, or consensus reality, such as with statements like,

Right on red *is* against the law here

The sun *is* shining

My name *is* Jill

That *is* the restaurant I mentioned earlier

However, when we use "is" or other forms of the verb "to be" (such as *are, am, were, was, should,* and *ought*) without such clear referents, we can wind up disempowered, disconnected from others, or worse. We can feel bad about ourselves. We can get into arguments, or even wars. Examples include when we argue about what "is" right or wrong, or who "is" bad, or even telling ourselves (or others) that we're "just 'being' silly (or dramatic, or immature)," dismissing our own feelings and intuition that arise from within. Such "is" examples abound unfettered throughout most human conversations and thoughts.

My aim here is not to categorically vilify this little word—we also have plenty of opportunities to use unreferenced "is" for good. For example, I still remember my childhood hero Mister Rogers saying, "You are special, and I like you just the way you are."

Swoon.

So no, *is* isn't the unequivocal enemy.

Rather, I want to equip us with the capacity to notice when we're using *is* and other forms of the verb *to be* against our own clear thinking, sense of empowerment, or values. Some examples could include,

We're doomed.

You are doing that wrong.

That person is not worth trying to talk to.

I'm a loser.

Those statements stop engagement by referencing a static description of reality. While they might invite agreement, disagreement, or argument, they do not invite deeper dialogue, creativity, or imagination. For most "is" statements like that, *there's a truer, more internally-referenced thing we can say* that opens up a further-reaching internal or external dialogue. The more internally-referenced our thoughts and utterances, the more power we have to resist the conversation-stopping effect of *is*. Conclusions for example, typically contain "is" statements, and a multiply-attributed quote goes, "A conclusion is the place where you got tired of thinking."

Here are some ways of translating those externally-referenced "is" statements above into more internally-referenced ones that invite the speaker of the phrase or thinker of the thought into a more dynamic relationship with what gave rise to the thought:

We're doomed.	I feel really scared and hopeless, and I can't see a way out right now.
I am not able to/suited for (fill in the blank)	I feel doubtful about whether I'll be able to do this thing.
That person is not worth trying to talk to	I feel wary about approaching them after our last conversation, and afraid of repeating that same unpleasant experience.
I'm a loser.	I feel sad about how I handled that situation, and I want to do better next time.

The statements in the right column above reference the internal state of the speaker, remove the static conclusion about reality that *is* delivers, and instead, invites more dynamic engagement.

Traditionally, oppressors deliberately override the inner experiences of the oppressed. As individuals, many of us in turn quash our own inner experiences, as we learned to do as children. Parenting, schooling, and language socialize us early and often to suppress and distrust our most basic feelings and needs, with admonishments like,

Stop crying—be a big boy/girl.

You aren't hungry, you just had a snack.

This isn't a big deal.

You're being disloyal to the family.

Or worse, being gaslit that abuse didn't really happen, or it wasn't really so bad. All these get doled out in the form of overt or hidden "is" statements.

Those examples appear as fractals, or pattern repetition at a smaller scale, of the larger phenomena of war, oppression, and other forms of power-over. In other words, when we use *is* to negate our own or others' larger, richer internal human realities, we reproduce the gestalt of genocide—we're saying this little piece of life, as it expresses itself in this moment, doesn't matter. So we snuff it out with *is*. When those fractal interactions proliferate, we have a populace ripe for subjugation.

The statements on the right side of table above invite deeper inquiry into our own and others' inner worlds, from which place we can source our commonalities, our power, our collective sense of possibility. As Audre Lorde famously articulated this in "Uses of the Erotic: The Erotic as Power,"

"When we live outside ourselves, and by that I mean on external directives only rather than from our internal knowledge and needs, when we live away from those erotic guides from within ourselves, then our lives are limited by external and alien forms, and we conform to the needs of a structure that is not based on human need, let alone an individual's."

Lorde's invocation of the erotic is not solely about sexuality but about the deep, intuitive knowing that resists dehumanization. She calls for a life lived from within, one that resists suffering, self-negation, and numbness. True resistance is not just defiant outward action, but also a profound, committed intimacy with our own inner compass.

For completeness's sake, I want to also mention how *is* can liberate by naming collective harmful phenomena so that victims can realize they're not alone. For example, when a worker feels uncomfortable with their manager repeatedly physically contacting them in an intimate way, they may brush away their own discomfort. Hearing from someone more experienced that this *is* sexual harassment and *is* illegal, can put them in touch with their own power to resist and act on their own behalf.

However, this moment of liberation can become an ideology that reverses into oppression, if we wield our own beliefs and ideology in ways that negate ourselves or others. This too is a fractal enactment of tyranny. When we cancel others because we "are right," this transforms nothing. We liberated ourselves from one ideology, and conscripted ourselves into another.

In college, I got disillusioned when I saw how feminism reproduced racism and classism within its ranks. I learned that most social and political theories fail to account for the power dynamics that ensue when followers of those theories attempt to carry them out. Marx famously on his deathbed said, "I am not a Marxist." Susan Griffin's "The Way of All Ideology" helped drive this home for me:

"When a theory is transformed into an ideology, it begins to destroy the self and self-knowledge. Originally born of feeling, it pretends to float above and around feeling. Above sensation. It organizes experience according to itself, without touching experience. By virtue of being itself, it is supposed to know. To invoke the name of this ideology is to confer truthfulness. No one can tell it anything new. Experience ceases to surprise it, inform it, transform it. It is annoyed by any detail which does not fit into its world view. Begun as a cry against the denial of truth, now it denies any truth which does not fit into its scheme. Begun as a way to restore one's sense of reality, now it attempts to discipline real people, to remake natural beings after its own image. All that it fails to explain it records as its enemy. Begun as a theory of liberation, it is threatened by new theories of liberation; it builds a prison for the mind."

Again, our individual imprisonment reproduces in microcosm the same oppressive gestalt we sought to oppose. No matter how liberatory, ideologies and theories carry an "is," which, without more dynamic practices, disconnect us from life. Walking our talk requires mutual, dynamic dances—embodied, linguistic *practices* of internal reference to recognize each other's humanity and discover how we impact each other moment-to-moment. To do that, we need "is" literacy in the first place—not as a replacement for direct action, but as a fundamental way to change the fractal reproduction of violence at the smallest level, to seed the whole.

Currently, *is*ism appears rampantly in how we dehumanize ourselves, others, and entire groups of people. With the United States now being run by a feudal oligarchy and threatening more harm every day, now is a perfect time to turn our attention to practicing more internally-referenced ways of thinking and communicating as embodied resistance to tyranny, from the inside out. This lays the groundwork for replacing division with solidarity; alienation with empowerment; and hopelessness with joy, and a sense of possibility.

Jill Nagle is a multiply-published author currently working on two books, *Hidden in Plain Sight*: *The Two-letter Word that Hijacks our Minds, and How to Reclaim Clarity, Connection, Freedom, and Joy*, and *Skin in the Game*: *How White People Benefit from Dismantling White Supremacy*. She's also working on an app to provide on-demand conflict resolution at Mendful.world.

A Quick Guide for the Everyday Protestor
By Jim Gialamas

I once asked my father why students were always the ones protesting. He told me, "Because the rest of us have jobs." For better or for worse, that's how we protest in America: students do the groundwork, while the rest of us write letters.

Unprecedented times require exceptional efforts.

Democracy is facing critical challenges. Government leaders are alternately callous or hapless. That puts the rest of us in the middle. It means that you have to speak up for what's right. Here's how a primer on getting started, based on my modest experience.

Find your people

You might have to kiss a few frogs. Advocacy groups vary in size and impact. Inquire among your socially conscious friends. Follow a few organizations on social media and attend live and virtual meetings.

Pick your issue

With so much happening, it's easy to feel overwhelmed. Consider what matters most to you and your loved ones. For me, it's protecting pre-existing conditions coverage under Obamacare.

Don't hold back

Start speaking to family, friends, and even— judiciously— professional contacts. You'll encourage like-minded people. I've found support from colleagues, my accountant, and even my financial advisor. Debates on social media with opposing viewpoints draw unexpected allies. You'll be surprised. Speak your mind, and you'll find your people.

Propriety wins the day

Statements like "Trump is a dumbass" only energize the opposition. Instead, focus on defining your issue. Present a reasoned argument. Avoid whataboutism and personal attacks. Stay on message and use clear talking points. They go a long way.

Expect warnings from friends and family

Sharing protest plans often draws comments like "be careful." One guy even told me, "Nothing good will come of it." So it's important to express your enthusiasm and report back on your progress.

Remember to invite your friends

Whether they attend or not, sharing the activity is part of your "base building." Protesting is new for many people so your job is to educate and encourage them. Don't forget to post photos.

Here's what to expect on a march

They last several hours. Wear weather-appropriate shoes. Conserve your energy and your patience. Bring water and snacks. Watch and learn.

Make advocacy a regular calendar entry

Schedule meetings and protests. While you're at it, buy some postcards and postage, and make sure you have contact information at the ready.

Protesting isn't easy, but it's essential. The time to act is now. You'll have some challenges, but you'll also make new friends and allies. Every step you take, adds to the collective effort.

Jim Gialamas has contributed to *The New York Times, Forbes, The South Carolina Review* and *Eclectica.* His spoken commentaries have appeared on the public radio program, Marketplace.

Technical fingerprint Expert-
Bureau of Criminal Investigations
By Deborah Hammonds

Growing up in a tumultuous era marked by significant social and political upheaval, my formative years were deeply influenced by the shifting landscapes of the 1960s and 1970s. The era was characterized by a relentless struggle for civil rights, a time when the clamor for equality and justice resonated through every corner of society. Despite the pervasive atmosphere of discrimination and hatred, my youthful mind remained largely insulated from the machinations of the political world. It wasn't until I embarked on a career in law enforcement that I began to grasp the inextricable link between politics and the operational dynamics of the system I was part of.

The position I held within the law enforcement agency served as a lens through which I observed the intricate interplay of power, policy, and influence. It was a revelation, albeit a sobering one, to witness firsthand how political agendas could steer the course of justice and governance. Yet, this immersion in the political realm did not foster a sense of engagement, but rather a growing disenchantment with the state of our democracy.

As I navigated the complexities of my profession, my perception of the political landscape evolved from one of naive detachment to a more nuanced understanding fraught with disappointment and frustration. The ideals of democracy seemed increasingly compromised by the very forces that were meant to uphold them.

In the midst of the societal advancements of 2025, it is disheartening to see that the specter of hatred and discrimination continues to loom large. The re-election of a polarizing figure has only served to embolden these regressive tendencies, making them more overt and pervasive.

In the ensuing years of these turbulent times, I will stay strong in my belief that love can overcome hate, that morality will return and in order to survive I will focus on the love of my family, I will raise my voice in protest against restricting the rights of women, social upheaval and most of all, hate. I will support the efforts for Health care, for Veterans' services and stand for what's right, I do not and will not tolerate disrespect, hate or injustice and will call it out to any and everyone who needs to hear it. My faith will always be in the forefront of all of my endeavors and pray for the hope of all mankind.

Deborah Hammonds has worked at the Sheriff's office for over 20 years as an Identification Officer specializing in fingerprinting and criminal Identification in the Bureau of criminal investigations (BCI), which she describes as a rewarding and learning experience that has given her firsthand insight into the importance of being part of a dynamic team that aids Sheriff's officers in the apprehension of wanted individuals.

Her other passion is the loves of her life, her son and grandson, who bring her joy each and every day.

Lift Every Voice
By Patt Mihailoff

Everyday resistance seems to have been part of my entire life in one way or another. There was always something going on that needed attention, not just mine, but everyone's if a difference was to be made.

It wasn't until November 8th, 2016 that I felt my entire voting history meant nothing. As I struggled to understand the following four years and thankfully made it through, I could not believe my lying ears or eyes when on January 20th, 2025, the same thing happened—AGAIN.

My mind went from where are all the women who had been insulted, disparaged and demeaned, to what are they thinking? I remember telling everyone who asked, *why do you vote?* And I answered, because Black AND white people died so that I can have that right and because it was my civic duty so that their deaths would not be in vain.

Every single day it was something different that triggered me. Every day for four years I was looking at someone I knew was not the right person to lead this nation, a nation that hadn't always been fair to me and mine, but it's the only country I want to live in. Even though there were people who disagreed with me, I stood fast in my defense of their right to disagree because this is supposed to be a democracy.

When I was young, I remember reading Ray Bradbury's *Fahrenheit 451* as well as seeing the movie, and while I was greatly entertained, I was convinced that something like that could *never* happen in this country. How wrong I was; as book banning started becoming the norm instituted by a few voices who screamed the loudest at what they all *suddenly* thought, *To Kill a Mockingbird, Of Mice and Men, The Kite Runner, The Bluest Eye*, and close to 40,000 other books were inappropriate.

I was beginning to see similarities between now and 1939. Suspicion, hate and division was consuming the United States of America as lies were spreading faster than the truth could get out of bed on a daily basis.

Long-time friends and acquaintances who I *thought* could see through the inconsistencies, the beginning of the breakdown of democracy and the total mind-blowing disregard of the Constitution, either fought me tooth and nail with inane and inaccurate rhetoric or ignored me altogether. It was sad as entire families became divided over it and some were not speaking or sharing holidays together anymore. How could this happen?

We all know that racism and bias has always been a part of society, there have been horrible instances throughout our history. We tried to maintain our trust in the institutions that were voted into service, the Senate, the House of Representatives and the Supreme Court only to bear witness to their absolute failure to uphold the oaths that they all swore to… all because of their fear of one man, a person who decided that he was to be the alpha and the omega.

My faith was on the brink of collapse, because none of my prayers had been answered. I cried, I complained, I got sick over all of it and on January 20th, 2025 when I saw a man who took an oath without placing his hand on the Bible his wife held, I knew that now was not the time to give up or give in.

We are going to get through this. We are going to have a hard fight ahead, but we will prevail, because there are decent human beings on both sides who will not let the fabric of this nation fall to dictatorship and anarchy.

So what's the plan?

We women will lift our voices high and loud and call out these injustices.

I will not shop at stores who will fall in line with the perceived notion of non-diversity.

I stand with our LBGTQ community.

I demand equal rights for all.

I will make calls and write letters to my senators and congressmen to make sure they know they were elected by the people and for the people, and not for personal gain or give in to fearmongering and threats. We will stand *with* them if they stand *for* us.

I will make sure that people understand that this is for all of us, not just some of us. Change cannot happen by itself; it will take the collective actions and voices of all of us to make sure that decency and the letter of the law is upheld for and by everyone.

So please join with me in lifting EVERY VOICE.

Patt Mihailoff writes in a wide range of genres including paranormal, erotica and short stories, but she has a particular affection for historical westerns, medieval stories with a twist and short stories. She has published over 200 in the TRUE CONFESSION series and their subsidiaries.

She has published in several anthologies for N.Y. Times Bestselling author Zane's anthologies, and as half of the writing duo P.K. Eden, which enjoyed receiving a five-star review in the country's leading review magazine, Affaire *De Coeur* for their novel FIREBRAND.

In 2009 Patt received the prestigious *Author of the Year Award* from the Romance Writers of America New York City chapter, followed by *Mentor of the Year* award in 2010. Patt also enjoys crocheting Lap robes and Prayer shawls which she donates to nursing homes, Veterans' Hospitals and Cancer centers in NJ and Del. and for anyone who wants one. She retired from her dream job at the NJ Sheriff's office and relocated to Delaware.

Fighting Back
By Michael A. Ventrella

This didn't just happen. This was a long term plan by a coalition of financial and Christian conservatives to subvert our democracy.

Part of this is the natural progression of society—those in power will do everything they can to keep the power, and no rights are ever given to others freely. We make progress and then there is a blowback and we fight back, and, given history, we do eventually win, but it's never easy.

In modern American history, this all started when Reagan was elected, and the conservatives suddenly realized that they could get away with a lot of shit. They sold arms to our enemies, and gave huge tax breaks to millionaires and made poor people pay taxes on their Social Security. And the window of discourse got moved to the right.

When George Bush senior ran against Michael Dukakis, he called Dukakis a "liberal" as if it was an insult, and liberals stupidly rebranded themselves as "progressives" and ran away from the liberal label instead of embracing it. And we moved farther to the right, while the rest of the civilized world went left.

One of the ways they get away with this is by filling the courts, which most people don't pay attention to, so when Bush junior lost the election, he got the Supreme Court to ignore the voters and place him in power. And more conservative judges were put in.

And each time, the conservatives realized they could cheat and lie and get away with crap because they were playing hardball with politics while we liberals clutched our hankies and refused to get in the mud and fight back.

So let's cut to the chase: What can we do now, with an idiot President who ignores the Constitution and a House, Senate and Supreme Court that cares little about "checks and balances" and allows all this to happen?

Obviously, the most important thing is (I know you hate to hear this) is to vote. They have spent decades doing everything they can to keep us from voting because they know when we all vote, they lose. And only vote for Democrats. Some liberals are so "pure" they don't understand that their protest votes for third party candidates or their refusal to vote at all is one of the reasons we are in this mess to being with. (Trump won in 2024 by less than 50%, mind you—if those third party people had voted for Harris, we wouldn't be in this mess. You have my permission to blame these people in the same way you blame clueless Trump supporters.)

But what we really need to do is put pressure on our representatives. Call them constantly. Phone calls are more important than emails or letters. Don't ignore those who support us—they need to be called too, to remind them that they need to do their job.

And here's the thing some people miss: You need to call your state politicians as well. Your governor, state house members, even local city elected officials The fight can be at the state level. We need to encourage them to say no to the federal government. We need a non-violent civil war here, with civil disobedience, with local governments refusing to allow the feds to come in and cause their destruction. We need to throw monkey wrenches into every bit of the federal political machinery.

And of course you need to financially support groups like the ACLU and unions and other groups that are actively fighting in the judicial system for our rights.

There are more of us than there are of them. Every public survey shows that our vision of America is supported by the majority of the population. Trump lost the popular vote the first time he ran, never even reached a 50% approval rating the entire time he was president. He lost the second popular vote by a bigger margin, and won this time with less than 50% of the vote (and has an even lower approval rating in the polls than last time). He has never had the support of a majority of Americans, and we need to constantly remind our politicians of that.

But none of that matters if we don't get involved and especially if we don't vote.

Michael A. Ventrella is an attorney and Constitutional Law professor who also writes humorous adventure novels. His book *How to Argue the Constitution with a Conservative* features cartoons from Pulitzer-Prize winner Darrin Bell and is available everywhere. His web page is www.MichaelAVentrella.com

Haiku
By Lynn Seftner

Poisonous dark words
Slip through cracks like deadly smoke
Our house is on fire

Peaceful cats slumber
While vicious rats destroy home
Time to unsheathe claws

Is this a bad dream?
The nightmare ends only when
I turn off the news

I am a groundhog
Tentative nose sniffs, retreats
Darkest days still here

Orange flames crackle
Burning down all we hold dear
His brain is on fire

Lynn Seftner is a retired career development specialist from the field of education.

During these troubled times, she finds hope and comfort in her faith. Micah 6:8 "What does the Lord require of you but to do justice, and to love kindness and to walk humbly with your God"

I Am Not Ok
By Domina

I think it is time for me to admit, the current state of affairs in the USA is affecting my mental and emotional health. If you look through my entire history and if you know me, I don't... feel the need to make a proclamation about my feelings, I don't post memes about "hang in there," I don't seek support from anyone on an emotional level. I tried not to "like" political things or get into political arguments.

But

I think the level of cruelty that has infected this country, from the bottom to the top and back down again, like a fucking fountain of hate, is fucking with me. I am not happy. A lot. I am discontented, a lot. It is a general sense of feeling off, feeling nervous, feeling sad.

I don't know whether to hope it all works out or that he burns this place to the ground so I can say, "I told you so."

Also

We all learned in school that Nazis were bad. And we learned the poem.

> *"First they came for the socialists,*
> *and I did not speak out—*
> *because I was not a socialist.*
> *Then they came for the trade unionists..."*

And we all see this happening now.

We shook our heads at the bystanders for allowing this to happen. "Never again!" we said. But what they didn't teach us is...

What were those bystanders supposed to do? What are we now supposed to do? We were taught to learn from history and never let it repeat, but they didn't teach us how.

I will join the national boycotts ? But is that going to do anything!?

MAGA members might be fucking cult members but at least they DID something. They stormed the castle to try and save democracy.

What are we doing!? No one taught us what to do.

They are murdering democracy. They are rounding up people. They are stealing our livelihoods. They are literally coming for the socialists and for the trade unionists. People are being fired by the thousands.

What are we supposed to do?!

Remember the lessons about the civil war... "neighbor against neighbor, brother against brother"?

"Can you imagine?" they asked us.

Yes, I can imagine it. Because it is happening. I have family members in the cult. It has strained our family relationships. My daughters have cried as my parents have lamented that this country is trying to "normalize" gay people.

I am so fucking angry and sad and scared and tired.

And I am a teacher. Do you read the news...?

First they came for the trans people,

then they came for the immigrants,

then they came for government workers...

Now they come for me.

Who will stand by and do nothing? Everyone. Even me.

Because we were never taught what to do.

Maybe this is why?

After writing the first draft of this essay, my editor said "I would really like it if you could add something at the end about trying to figure out how to resist."

But... this was a writing about my frustration and despair. If I knew how to resist I wouldn't be crying out to the void for guidance. But, ever the people-pleaser, I gave it a try.

To try and find some answers I looked outward to see what others were doing.

I was immediately drawn to the mindset of Veteran Democratic strategist James Carville who said "It's time for Democrats to embark on the most daring political maneuver in the history of our party: roll over and play dead,". Boy is that tempting. Do nothing. Let them burn this place to the ground. Be smug in the ashes. Stick a "Not My President" sticker on my car and gloat.

But, gloating while my daughters and I have lost the right to control our bodies and cannot get jobs because... you know... DEI is wrong, and we have no social support like Medicare or unemployment to help us, seems like a hollow victory.

At the same time, Illinois Gov. J.B. Pritzker said, "It took the Nazis one month, three weeks, two days, eight hours and 40 minutes to dismantle a constitutional republic... when the five-alarm fire starts to burn, every good person better be ready to man a post with a bucket of water if you want to stop it from raging out of control."

This seems to have more of the urgency and outrage I am looking for, but again, short on specifics.

I guess Maine Sen. Angus King said it best, "We're in uncharted territory. There's no playbook for this... Everybody's trying to figure out what's effective."

Which takes us right back to... What do we do?

Here is what some people are doing...

Some judges have pushed back at his "executive orders."

In Seattle, U.S. District Judge John Coughenour blocked Trump's executive order on birthright citizenship. In Boston, U.S. District Judge George O'Toole Jr. paused Trump's plan to encourage federal workers to resign by offering them paid leave.

And in that group are also the lawyers and plaintiffs taking on these cases, taking on personal risk from maga fanatics. (Has anyone noticed I refuse to capitalize "trump" or "maga" and recently "vance"?)

There are also the National Park Service X accounts that went sharing climate change facts that were censored. This led to the creation of an alternative account, @AltNatParkSer, which described itself as "The Unofficial 'Resistance' team of the U.S. National Park Service." This account quickly gained more followers than the official one.

And

The American Federation of Government Employees reports to its members what is REALLY going on. Due to this disclosure of truth, workers are filing lawsuits, participating in protests, and sharing internal documents with the media. They've created anonymous websites and social media accounts to spread their messages, developed resource guides, and recorded private meetings. In some cases, they've resigned in large numbers to protest Musk and the U.S. DOGE Service.

OK. but I am not a politician, or judge, or lawyer or federal worker. What can I do? Well, this is what the internet recommends:

"Do not allow the normalization of Trump."

I take this to mean, speak out wherever I can, wherever I can, to whomever I can.

"Advocacy groups and everyday citizens must become a unified blocking force for Congressional Democrats who are fighting against Trump's extreme agenda."

I gotta be honest, this is what I did in the first place and it sparked my depression and anxiety. I joined my local Democratic party and… at 53 years old, I was the youngest in the room. It was chaos, it was out of date, and out of touch. It was the beginning of my thought process that… we will never beat "the machine" that is maga.

BUT

There is the advice. Maybe you will have a better experience with it than I did.

"Become as invested in the Midterm Elections as you were in the Presidential, as if your life depended on it."

I mean, in theory, anyone can run, anyone can work on a campaign, and AS OF NOW, most of us can vote.

This next one is a little more ballsy, maybe you have seen some of this on TikTok or even in the news…

"Call them out in public, at town halls, in their district offices, and on their phone lines. Demand to know… Force them to take a stance. Put them on record. Make them say it out loud."

U.S. Senator Susan Collins from Maine announced that she will oppose President Donald Trump's attempt to withhold federal funding from the state due to the Maine Principals' Association's decision to permit transgender student-athletes to participate in girls' sports, TO HIS FACE.

In northern Idaho, three plainclothes security workers forcibly removed Teresa Borrenpohl from a legislative town hall meeting when she yelled out "Is this a town hall, or a lecture?"

This style of rebellion seems right up my alley. Snark, bravery, and little prep time. Just a deep breath and your truth.

And finally..

Ensure voters never forget. Make sure the names of the guilty are everywhere in their district. Every voter should be fully aware of who betrayed them and who is accountable for the fallout.

Show up both online and in person. Expose their complicity—call them out on social media, overwhelm local news with letters and op-eds, and take action in their districts. Let them know we're paying attention.

So, how is that for an ending? Did I inspire? Are you planning your course of action right now?

In truth, what I did for myself was look at my stress and I made a list of all the things that were causing it. Then I choose one thing that I have control of, and I made a choice about that. And I took some steps towards bettering my life in that small way.

And things felt better.

So now, I am taking another step. I am focusing on positivity. I am at work, doing my best, and spreading positivity. And if I am successful and remove this stress of negative thinking from my life, I will take another step and another step, slowly making changes in small ways, that will hopefully lead to a better mental state, a better life, and maybe even a better world.

The author is a lifestyle domme who lives with her submissive in Cleveland, Ohio. She found herself through kink and lives her truth. She has been an educator for 35 years.

My Resistance Playbook
By Dr. Nathasha Brooks-Harris

I vividly recall walking down Brooklyn's Nostrand Avenue on a beautiful and sunny day, one late morning with my mother. Hand in hand, we walked. We ended up at a center that was dark and musty. My mother let go of my hand long enough for her to go into her purse and retrieve her voting card that identified her and proved that she was registered Democrat. She gave it to a white man behind the table who seemed indifferent. He examined her card and proceeded to ask her a lot of questions—which she answered in a polite, but stern manner. She had voted many times before since she had arrived in New York in 1945 during the Great Migration. This time was different. None of the answers she had answered were good enough to the man. He kept asking more, and she kept answering. He even asked her to read something—which she did with fluency. Eventually, someone saw what he was doing and intervened: perhaps, a supervisor or someone with the power to stop him. She was cleared to go into the booth and vote. She grabbed my hand and into the booth we went. I remember looking around the booth at all the tiny levers, the curtain, and the large lever she pulled when she cast her vote.

This was before the passage of The Voting Rights Act of 1965. The year was 1961 and I was a four-year-old filled with thoughts that I would one day go into a similar voting booth and vote. However, I hoped that it would be without the drama she had gone through.

Although that happened over 60 years ago, it seems like yesterday, and the memory haunts me to this day. I remember how my parents—both Southerners—recalled not being able to vote with ease because of having to take literacy tests, pay a poll tax, and having the Grandfather Clause quoted to them. They often talked about how much blood was shed by people who fought for the rights of Black people (called "colored" or Negro back then) to vote. My parents said that Black people contributed well to

109

society, paid taxes, and lived life like their white counterparts, so they deserved the right to vote and have a say in who was running the country and making decisions that affected all Americans. Voting was something they took seriously and were passionate about. They did not let an election go by without voting and were often there when the polling place doors opened. I am not sure why my mother went without my father that day or why she went later than usual.

That incident never happened again. My parents always went to vote together at the crack of dawn. I believe that it was the passage of the Voting Rights Act of 1965 that afforded them the right to vote. They instilled in me the importance of voting and made sure that I saw plenty of documentaries and read plenty of books about the Jim Crow South and how Black people were denied the right to vote and were beaten or killed for trying. In fact, when I was grown and married and relocated to Pennsylvania, my father wrote me lectures in their letters about not forgetting to vote and how our people fought and died for my/our right to vote. Then he continued the lecture during our phone calls. Even if I didn't feel like voting, I didn't have the option. My parents' voices were too strong in my head and got me up and moving.

No one could have told me that when the Voting Rights Act of 1965 expired in 2015 it would not be extended or renewed. It seemed that little care was taken to ensure that this important piece of legislation stayed active and on the books. In fact, I won't ever forget how the Southern states were champing at the bit after it expired. They dusted off the literacy tests and probably had visions of reinstating poll tax and the Grandfather Clause. I had assumed that the protection of this legislation would continue to protect us, but I was so wrong.

Things continued to go downhill with the election of Donald J. Trump as president. He came into the White House and showed himself as racist, homophobic, xenophobic, and narcissistic. All of his rhetoric emboldened hate groups and made people feel entitled to practice racism and exclusionary practices across the United States. I suppose they thought if the "leader" of our country could do such evil things, why couldn't they? As if that wasn't bad enough, he tried everything to silence Dr. Fauci from telling us about what was happening with Covid so we could stay alive. Forty-five (I do not call that man's name) did not take the mask mandate or anything related to Covid seriously. Hundreds of thousands of people died during the pandemic because there was no treatment, only ventilators. He distanced himself from any and everything that would help Americans stay alive and not die from Covid. He could care less about funding a vaccine to save us and incited division amongst people about getting it if one was to be created. Instead, he gave us a deadly recipe of household agents for us to drink as a cure. However, when he had Covid, he went to the hospital and was given treatment not available to us. Three days later, he was fine—walking on the balcony at the White House and giving a press conference talking nonsense. Meanwhile, Americans continued dying.

Fast forward to 2025 and he was inaugurated as president of the United States for the second time. His first go-round was bad, but this time feels worse than before. He told us exactly what he would do when he was reelected, and he has not deviated from it. He clearly said when he got back into the White House, he would never leave, and we would not have to ever vote again. He explained how we would go from a democracy to a dictatorship (not actually calling it that, but everyone knew what it was), but no one believed because they were too concerned with getting President Biden out because he was too old, rising prices, and deporting the migrants. They were too distracted by Felon 47's Madison Square Garden rally that mimicked the Nazi rally there in 1939 to care that he would take the country in the wrong direction as many of his proposed policies and ideologies mimicked Hitler's. The handwriting was on the proverbial wall that our new "president" would change America into something unrecognizable and into a place where we wouldn't want to live.

On his first day, he set America back decades by signing 75 Executive Orders that reversed Diversity, Equity, and Inclusion (DEI), women's rights, gender equality, gay and lesbian rights, and streamlining the federal government workforce by closing whole agencies and gutting others. ICE began immediately deporting migrants. Many places became a police state with ICE running rampant—and this was still Day One.

Right after that, planes began to drop out of the sky. He had fired essential air traffic controllers who were already low in number and overworked. Recently the new Secretary of Health and Human Services, Robert F. Kennedy Jr., said he would create camps in which to put mentally ill people. That was the beginning of what looked like a replica of *1984*, George Orwell's seminal novel about society's descent into dystopia. America was slowly becoming a dystopian society and each day it was getting worse. The question is: how did we allow a convicted felon to man the highest office in the land? How exactly did this go over our heads and happen? We are seeing the downfall of democracy into fascism with each Executive Order he signs. Please remember that it took Adolph Hitler 53 days to thrust Germany from a democratic society into a fascist society. Do let that sink in!

This White House is like a three-ring circus as there is an environment of chaos and confusion to distract from the felon's and Musk's and DOGE's antics. We don't know what they're doing or what will happen next. While they distracted us with their buffoonery, they removed the traditional American flag off the Federal government agency websites such as the FBI's site and others and replaced it with a nine-star America flag, the Confederate flag! The prices of food have skyrocketed. Shelves are empty in some markets because of supply issues and issues from the tariffs he imposed on some countries. The bottom line is that he is undoing all the rights and protections that our ancestors fought and died for, and we are slowly but most assuredly, moving back into segregation and Jim Crow. That will come next. His agenda is straight out of Project 2025 (now called 2025 Presidential Transition Project—as if we're stuck on stupid), which will be carried out by his cabinet of incompetency.

We, as American people, cannot allow this travesty of governmental power and control to happen on our watch. It is incumbent that resistance must happen, and we must do something to maintain our democracy and ensure that our Constitution will be followed. To that end, I will use those things "in my hand," to develop my resistance playbook, just as God asked Moses what was in his hand when he told him to deliver the Israelites out of Egypt, but Moses was reluctant because he didn't speak well. God told him to use what was in his hand and He would use him as necessary to get the job done. That task would be rooted in faith. I will use the tools in my hand: art, writing and editing, teaching and communication. My playbook, with God's help, will consist of the following:

I will create quilts, dolls, and fiber art pieces that have messages of resistance. I will channel the energy that the Chilean women used in creating Arpilleras (miniature dolls in scenes depicted on burlap) to protest their government, as well as that of the Columbian women who told the stories of their suffering because of their political situation on colorful cloth wall hangings to tell our stories of what's happening now in America as I am led in my spirit.

I will use my voice as an author and writer to write about our current political situation as much as I can when given the opportunity to do so. The message is what matters most as these are dire times, and it needs to reach the masses. I will also use my editing skills to help publications get the message out, as plainly as possible, to the people.

I will incorporate some of the lessons from the now-banned Critical Race Theory/Black History syllabus into the curriculum when I teach my students. For example, I taught them about Juneteenth and Black History that happened in New York City that they were not aware of, and they appreciated it. I can embed that and other gems of knowledge within my classes.

Finally, I will use my voice to communicate with people across the globe via social media. When they darkened Tik Tok for 12 hours, the algorithm was changed, and new servers were installed that gave us For You pages that were not what we chose. However, an unintended consequence of their action made WorldTok, the pages of users around the world, now available to us. We could not see their pages or communicate with them before the blackout. They are reaching out to us to tell us that they are protesting in their countries on our behalf, and they stand with us. I communicate with users in Germany, Canada, England, Scotland, and Spain when I visit there in March to keep the lines of communication open to hear what they have to say and to thank them for their support. I am a culture and history buff, so I am learning a lot about these things, as well as their cuisine. It is all quite interesting that that new horizon has opened.

I feel a heavy tugging on my shoulders to help and resist where I can, using the tools in my hand, and not letting my ancestors down. They fought and died and endured great pain to make sure that my and their descendants have a softer life. I am their wildest dream having had three successful careers in publishing and journalism, public service in local government, and teaching (I am still teaching and am a proud professor). In 2020, a new platform for my art was placed in my path. I never saw it coming and know there's a reason. With God's help and divine providence, I kept their dream of getting a good education alive and completed my PhD in 2017 with a straight 4.0 average and admission into several honor societies. When I was hooded, I felt the presence of my ancestors around me cheering me on, telling me to go forth and make good trouble with those blessings. In that vein, I will do just that by using what's in my hand to help effect social change. It will take faith and divine guidance, but I am ready and up for the job—whatever needs to be done. Amen and ase'.

Nathasha Brooks-Harris enjoys telling stories in fabric and words. Her training in the Elder Craftsmen program and studying with an array of dollmaking and quilting teachers, including Helen Layfield, Elinor Peace Bailey, Susanna Oroyan, Sherry Goshon, Lesley O'Leary and others, prepared her for this artistic journey.

Brooks-Harris is the author of several romance novels and hundreds of short stories, as well as was formerly a magazine editor and entertainment journalist. She is currently an Adjunct Professor of Writing, Art Appreciation, and Human Services classes.

Brooks-Harris holds an MFA in Creative Writing from Spalding University, a Master of Science in Urban Studies from Queens College, and a PhD in Public Administration from Walden University.

In her spare time, she attends art programs for older adults, as well as teaches various fiber arts classes to senior citizens.

Brooks-Harris lives and works in Brooklyn, New York and is an avid traveler.

The Trump Blitz
by Carolyn Faggioni

The blitzkrieg, German for *lightning war,* was a military strategy used by Nazi Germany at the onset of World War II. This form of warfare was characterized by a rapid, highly coordinated assault designed to quickly overwhelm a country's defenses. Within months Poland, Denmark, Norway, Netherlands, Belgium, and France were conquered, falling under Nazi occupation.

Less than a month into Trump's second term, we've witnessed a political blitzkrieg of executive orders, proclamations, and mandates, including the firing of more than a dozen inspectors general, the watchdogs of various executive agencies. Some will say that this type of policy change is routine—that there is always a torrent of executive orders and personnel changes when an administration of the opposite party comes to power. While there is some truth to this, the magnitude and rapidity of this onslaught has created a seismic shift across the nation, evoking fear and a sense of hopelessness in many.

Trump's political blitz is about overwhelming the opposition in order to make sweeping change. The pardoning of nearly 1500 January 6th rioters including those that violently assaulted police officers, the threat of mass deportation of thousands of migrants, the delegitimization of transgender individuals, the withdrawal from both the Paris Climate Accord and the World Health Organization (WHO), the silencing of Department of Health officials as the bird flu spreads across the nation, the dismantling of federal DEI programs including those dating back to the 1960s and dedicated to ensuring the most basic civil rights protections, the stripping of federal security details for Dr. Fauci and other former federal government officials who had been critical of Trump, have had a devastating effect on many. Of course, that is the purpose of a blitzkrieg. The onslaught is so rapid and pervasive that the opposition loses the will to fight. Resistance is viewed as futile.

Migrants, Capitol Hill police, transgender individuals, and federal government workers, both past and present, may currently be in the frontlines, bearing the brunt of this onslaught, but those of us in the trenches will also feel the impact of this blitz in the weeks, months, and years to come.

Reversing efforts to combat climate change, raising tariffs on trading partners, and withdrawing from the World Health Organization are just a sampling of Trump policies that will have far reaching negative impacts not only on all Americans, but globally.

The Trump blitz has left elected officials and activists scrambling, not sure how and where to put up roadblocks, never mind launching a counteroffensive. Some will demand a widespread response that seeks to address as many issues as possible while others will argue something more concentrated, aimed at a few Trump policies, has greater efficacy. Infighting among Democratic officials and activists will make the resistance less effective, emboldening Trump and those that support his policy agenda. This must not happen. A dedicated and unified resistance, drawing upon the example and methods of individuals like Dr. Martin Luther King Jr. whose birthday we celebrated this past inauguration day, must emerge to counter Trump. As Dr. King had said, "The time is always right, to do what is right." That time is now.

Carolyn Faggioni is a retired high school social studies teacher from New York State. In Carolyn's 39 year career she has taught numerous courses including Advanced Placement United States Government and Politics and World History. Carolyn is committed to defending our democracy, promoting civic engagement, and social justice. Carolyn has recently launched a newsletter *Ascent with Carolyn* on Substack.

Next Gen
By Louisa Bacio

I'm married to a Republican. It's a dirty little secret in my liberal world. He's retired Air Force, and his father worked in law enforcement. We are figments of our ancestry.

I broke free, though, from the conservative mindset of my extended family. I like to explain that he's fiscally conservative but socially liberal. He believes that people should be able to live their lives as they want, which includes gay marriage and acceptance of all gender identity.

When Hillary lost the presidential race to Trump, he brought me a glass of wine as I cried in the bathtub. He assured me it would be all right, and maybe for our insular world, it was... but not for the greater good.

Cracks formed with the death of Ruth Bader Ginsburg. The pit of despair in my stomach grew.

My biggest resistance: We've spawned two Democrats and at 18 and 22, we can outvote him on any issue.

"I don't understand how he's not concerned about... (fill in the blank)," the 18-year-old asks. "How can he not support rights for us?"

I like to think it's because we're isolated in California, but there's also the feeling of the greater good. Others need help, too.

On the night of the presidential election, my youngest and I wore Madam President T-shirts, Taylor Swift bracelets for Harris-Walz, and lamented that in her lifetime, she'd see a female president.

I hope.

Since selling her first short story in 2010, **Louisa Bacio** published more than 50 novels, novellas and short stories with 16 publishers (at last count!) in contemporary and paranormal romance.

A Southern California native, Bacio can't imagine living far away from the ocean. The multi-published author of romance enjoys writing within all realms.

Bacio shares her household with a supportive husband, two young adults and a multitude of pets. In her other life, she teaches college classes in English, journalism and popular culture.

Contact Details:

Website http://www.louisabacio.com
Facebook: http://www.facebook.com/louisabacio
https://www.facebook.com/Louisabacioauthor/
X: http://www.twitter.com/louisabacio
Instagram: http://www.Instagram.com/LouisaBacio

Letter to My Daughters
By Peg Shaw

After the 2016 election I wrote this letter to my daughters. Our country had lost its way. When my daughters turned to me for strength, I had to find it even when I didn't have it. But I've watched them find their way - both working hard to lift people up as best as they can. Young people give me a glimmer of hope. This letter reminds me of our original despair, and here we are again. But this time we stand firm—we are not going back.

All your life I have tried to protect you—introducing you to the world little by little: big, beautiful, light, sound, love. Then when you were ready: a complicated place where ideas and values clash, things are not always as they appear, and bad things happen. And so, this time is heart wrenching for me on so many levels. Like it or not, ready or not, the curtain is pulled back and all is exposed: hate, anger, greed. so ugly. and all I can say is I'm sorry.

I'm sorry you worry about living among hateful people. I'm sorry you fear for your friends who for many reasons are feeling so vulnerable, so targeted. I'm sorry it feels like too many men and women just said its ok to treat women as objects. I'm sorry you cry because our country just elected a man who mocks people with disabilities—-people you care about so deeply. I'm sorry it feels hopeless to care about our planet. I'm sorry you are scared for the future.

But although it may not feel like it right now—-you are stronger than you used to be. You've experienced an election of hope. and one of despair. You grasp the breadth of people good and bad. You appreciate the long arc of people fighting for what's right since way before you were born. You know your tribe.

And I need you to know that I am not sorry that you are deeply caring strong willed young women who are now angry, afraid, and cry. The world needs people exactly like you. So my hope is that you eventually find solid ground, take a deep breath, and go high - always lifting others with you.

Remember light, sound, and love,
Mom

Peg Shaw is an artist incorporating writing, video, sound, and photography. Her work translates, re-imagines, weaves, and layers concepts from family history, the memory of place, storytelling, and the filtered experience of living in a chaotic political time.

Born in Oak Park, IL, Shaw received an MFA in Photography from the School of the Art Institute of Chicago and is a Professor in Photography/Video at Parkland College in Champaign, IL. She lives in the woods in a timber-frame home they built by hand, where she works in her studio, writes stories, practices drums, protests/resists, and plants trees.

Me and the Hummingbird
By Sidney Burris

I was minding my own business the other morning, and my business was drinking coffee and grading exams on my laptop. My cell phone was leaning against the second screen attached to the laptop while Frank Sinatra was singing through that phone about how lonely he was. Frank, by the way, was a very lonely guy. Me too, particularly when I'm grading exams.

But I saw a notice from *The New York Times* scroll across the top of the phone, just above Frank himself who was sitting at a bar looking, well, lonely.

The headline read: "Scientists study the flight of hummingbirds to design robots for drone warfare."*

I don't typically feel called upon to defend hummingbirds whenever our military-industrial complex shows up. But this was different. Memories were at stake. Memories of sitting on my deck last summer when a ruby-throated hummer darted by my head, came to a dead stop a yard away, wheeled up and over backwards, drifted slowly down like a falling leaf and hovered at eye level, as mystified by my lumpish immobility as I was overjoyed by his dazzling maneuverability. That's what happened, and I'm as clear about it as any reasonable definition of the word "clear" will allow.

But I'm also equally clear about this: I don't want a hummingbird-robot designed for drone warfare intruding on the space the bird and I peacefully occupied for a few salvaging seconds. For the moment, we shared a habitable and peaceful life, and I cannot be persuaded to underestimate our time together. We've just reached the quarter-century mark of the new millennium, and I need whatever salvation I can get. From where I sat, the future looked troublesome enough, and this *Times* article wasn't helping.

I knew this, however: I needed more of these encounters in my life, if I were to resist the coming miseries, deprivations, and embarrassments streaming from the White House.

I'm not against envying members of the animal kingdom for their talents and strengths. Ever since I was a high-school miler, the cheetah has occupied an outsized place in my imagination. However, as each of the four laps of that event ended, and my cumulative times were screamed out to me by a gruff, red-faced man holding a stopwatch, so too did my cheetah-dreams come to a close.

Or even younger, as a boy climbing trees, I watched movies and documentaries showing chimpanzees swinging eloquently from limb to limb and tree to tree. I so envied them that I found a line of sapling pines near my house, climbed the first one, started the tree swinging back and forth by shifting my weight to increase its arc until I'd almost reached the next one in line, at which point, I leapt toward it and grabbed the first limb that I could. The limb promptly snapped, I fell, bounced off another limb or two on the way down, and finally fell on my back, looking up at a confusion of sapling, limb, pine needles, and sky. I never again mistook my tree-climbing abilities for those of a chimpanzee.

Leonardo da Vinci left behind sketches for an "ornithopter" flying machine based on his observation of birds. No one knows if he ever assembled it, or if he did, if it worked. If he did, I suspect it didn't. Currently, at Stanford University, Professor Mark Cutkosky has developed a lizard-like robot that can climb walls. Its feet use a "dry adhesion" that Professor Cutkosky adapted from a gecko's foot pads. At the Korea Research Institute of Ship and Ocean Engineering, Bong-Huan Jun and his co-workers have manufactured an underwater robot to help with salvage and rescue operations, particularly in strong currents where its crab-like, jointed legs make it more stable. Like a crab.

And speaking of cheetahs, The Defense Advanced Research Projects Agency, or DARPA, has successfully assembled the Boston Dynamics' Cheetah robot. It is the fastest quadruped robot in the world, and its designers see it as an agile and speedy asset on the battlefield.

We love animals, we envy animals, and we want to be more like them, particularly when we can create machines based on them that make our very own human lives more adaptable, less human. We've been looking at members of the animal kingdom with envy and wonder for millennia. I'm thinking of the cave paintings at Lascaux, France. They're 15,000 years old.

But maybe other animals deserve our attention. Especially now, as the fabric of our communities is being shredded. Like the dwarf mongoose, for example, who lives in stable family groups headed by the top female. Her mate, who is strictly monogamous, is second in command and serves as a lookout for the kinds of trouble that arise in sub-Saharan Africa. The female in command gets fed first, and then the youngest ones eat. Leaders first, and then, and only then, the up-and-coming generation next.

And orcas? They live together in pods ranging in size from five to 50 members, and the older ones work together as a coherent unit to educate the youngsters in the ways of the water they'll spend the rest of their lives navigating. And navigating together, I should tell you, as a family unit.

And of course prairie dogs. Their social organization is stunning. Their living quarters are hidden underground with separate chambers for sleeping, going to the bathroom, and showing the pups how to become generous and compassionate adults. After all, they share their food, groom one another, kiss and nuzzle, and generally make a public display of their warm devotion to the whole colony. And all of these animals have reached this level of co-operation without a single committee meeting.

I don't know what cheetahs would think about DARPA if they developed the capacity to do it, but personally, I'd like to see a little less DARPA and little more prairie dog in the planning for our collective future on an ailing planet.

It's not so hard to imagine. We need to understand at the deepest level the idea of community. Maybe pin it to the top of our to-do list. We need to see as clearly as we can the kinds of social disfigurement and the oppressive policies that compromise and question the deep reserves of compassion that we all carry within us.

I do not think that we are a broken people. But I do believe that people now are broken, that part of being a people lies in healing together our brokenness, our problems, our anxieties, our neuroses. And we do this, I also believe, in two ways: through individual self-knowledge, which I'll let you define however you wish, and through the deliberate creation of communal joy. You can also define "communal" however you wish—two or four or 40,000 folks doing something in harmony works for me—but be careful with "joy." Call it joy only if it ennobles or elevates or quiets or eases our troubled spirits. Call it joy if it brings us together, if only for a moment, and shows us that the things that hold us together outnumber by a long shot those that tear us apart. And shows us this with the force and clarity of a hummingbird suspended in mid-air on a deck. The kind of force and clarity that change us.

Because we need to change. Every single one of us. Get yourself in a peaceful place, have a seat, listen to the chatter, and you'll see why I say this. The amount of venom, spite, anger, one-upmanship, gotcha-talk, condescension, intolerance, propaganda, truth masquerading as Truth … invective, division … it's constant, it's unrelenting, and if you're not aware of it, and if you don't see the wounding that's happening to all of us, and if you don't find your own ways to heal it, then like me, you'll start listening to Nick Drake's final and darkest album, *Pink Moon* (1972) on constant rotation. And you don't want to be like me, because then you'll notice the rotation is not really a rotation, it's a downward spiral, the kind of spiral that Drake did so well and with such dangerous beauty. And there you go, like me, spiraling downward, beautifully dangerous. It's a mess.

But praise be to hummingbirds. Daniel Siegel, a psychiatrist and distinguished scholar of our wayward minds, came up with an idea I revisit continually whenever my moon turns pink. He speaks of our "interpersonal neurobiology," a regal phrase that simply means that our brains and minds operate independently of nothing. We operate, in fact, interdependently with everything: happy people, sad people, light breezes, heavy traffic, loud noises, quiet footfalls. The fall of a sparrow. The fate of a nation. Everything makes us, finally, who we are—neurobiologically, psychologically, politically, spiritually, mundanely, transcendentally. "Interpersonal neurobiology," Seigel claimed in a conversation with Gabor Maté, "is both a way of understanding the world through many disciplines, and it is also the reality of our interconnected nature."

I accept and proclaim, here and now, the discipline of the hummingbird. That beautiful, inquisitive, airborne, balletic spirit I encountered on my deck—we actually encountered each other—is now part of my interconnected nature.

That little bird taught me to leave well enough alone when it's time to leave well enough alone. To come, to see, to go. To flit, to look, to somersault with my ideas, to land lightly on my conclusions because someone else's ideas and conclusions just got their own set of wings too. And they will fly and finally land somewhere, maybe near me, maybe not, but we each will be left, before we die, with our little loops and flights that everything and everyone helped us to make. And these actions must bring us joy. They simply must. And so we undertake these actions in communion with our planet and with every living being that calls it home. I learned this heavy lesson from a bird that weighs seven grams.

The only logical conclusion to this is thanksgiving and praise. The only logical action to come from thanksgiving and praise is to protect, at all costs, our right to joy. Our right to the political institutions and social customs that guarantee the pursuit of joy to anyone who seeks it. Sacrifice these things, as I believe we are currently in danger of doing, and we sacrifice one of the most potent tools we have to resist whatever we feel needs to be resisted.

I'm thinking now, without apology, of hummingbirds. And of the joy they bring me. These too are the tools of change and resistance. To say that the hummingbird knew this during our encounter on my deck would be an overstatement. But to say that this tiny bird inspired in me the kind of disruptive joy that can't be controlled, that edges me closer to celebration and an inch or two away from conformity and so becomes the nightmare of all who seek to control us and to force us into a misshapen conformity, well, that is dead-on accurate.

And now that I think of it, dead-on accuracy is what all of us, no exceptions, need right now.

* "On the Wings of War," Jim Robbins, *The New York Times, Nov. 26, 2024.* https://www.nytimes.com/2024/11/26/science/hummingbirds-robots-drone-warfare.html

Sidney Burris' essays have appeared in *Five Points, The Virginia Quarterly Review, Agni, The Georgia Review, Southern Review, Shenandoah, Sewanee Review, Contemporary Literature,* and other journals. Three were in *Best American Essays* as Notable Essays (2002, 2004, 2008). Burris' poems have appeared in *The Atlantic, Poetry, The Harvard Review, Kenyon Review, Journal of American Poetry, The Virginia Quarterly Review, Prairie Schooner, Southern Review, Blackbird, Best American Poetry* (1996), and other journals.

Burris has published a book of literary criticism on Seamus Heaney and three books of original poetry. Along with a Tibetan monk at the University of Arkansas, Burris directed an oral-history project, The TEXT Program, that chronicles online the stories of Tibetans currently living in exile in India, and has taught, with the same monk, a course in the history and practice of nonviolence to unruly college students.

What Is Everyday Resistance to Me, and You?
By Lori Perkins

If you are reading this second edition of this book, you know that this book is one of my forms of everyday resistance. It was put together in a mere six weeks, collecting essays, cartoons and poetry from all over the country (and the world—we have one author living in Australia!).

The book has done well—we made the Amazon #1 best seller list in the categories of Constitution and Federal Government out of the starting gate, but some reviewers, more accustomed to reviewing books that were planned and scheduled 18 months in advance (which is the publishing industry norm) expressed regret that there were not more concrete examples of everyday resistance.

As someone who has been monitoring this topic, and doing this every day, I will try to highlight some of the ways you can resist every-day—and share some of the ways I resist on a daily basis. Individually they may not seem that powerful, but together we can accomplish multitudes (as seen in the collapse of the Tesla market not only in America, but throughout most of the world).

So, boycotts work.

Big, group boycotts like the one against Target (for its anti-DEI practices and diminishing of its LGBTQ support and moving its Pride merchandise to the back of the store), and the week-long Amazon boycott.

But small boycotts work too. Every time I go out of my way not to buy a Goya product for the brand's support of Trump, I feel better about myself (and I make a lot of Latin food). There's a list of beers I won't order because of Trump-supporting owners and/or campaign contri-butions (all Samuel Adams brands, Coors, Yuengling, just to name a few). And there's also brands I go out of my way to buy now because I know they are pro-FDEI and/or progressive, such as Costco and Apple.

You can also support a brand or a product or a person you agree with. As soon as I read that E. Jean Carrol, the woman who sued Trump for sexual assault and won twice, had written a "secret book," I bought a copy so that the book will place as high as possible on the best-seller list (BTW, she has yet to receive a penny of the $83 million payment that Trump owes her because he keeps on trying to move and/or re-litigate the case—fat chance as long as it stays in New York, where we all knew who he was a long time ag— just Google "Bonwit Teller façade preservation").

I was trained as a journalist. I have a degree in journalism from NYU where I taught undergraduate journalism and even owned a neighborhood newspaper in New York City, so I truly believe in the fourth estate, but I gave up on corporate journalism a long time ago. It is imperative that you keep informed. Do not give up on information.

I read the news online every day, but I stopped going to *The New York Times, The Washington Post* and *The LA Times* when thy showed up at Trump's inauguration and I learned that their CEO's all contributed to his campaign. Now I start my day with the Associated Press, which is free and much less opinionated.

I still read the various papers I mentioned, but I don't pay for them. I got an AppleOne subscription (annual is cheapest) that gives me access to all of the above, as well as many other magazines I like to read.

Before I discovered the AppleOne subscription, I would get around a paywalled article in corporate media by Googling "how to get around a paywall" (sometimes you have to ask Google for the specific work-around for that publication), and it always worked. I have always considered that everyday rebellion.

I also keep a journal. Have done that since I was 17, but it is more important now than ever in my life… and yours. If you ever kept a journal, start again. Online or on paper. Just write it all down, so you don't forget, and we don't forget.

I have chosen to be active on social media, so I'm on BlueSky, Facebook, Instagram, X (yes, because I still have a lot of followers there) and even LinkedIn. I am very vocal about what I believe and like, but I don't waste my time trolling and or with trolls. I'm on social media to see what the social discourse is, as well as to let anyone who cares know what I am doing/thinking.

In the next edition of this book (and unfortunately, I am fearful that there will be many, but I had originally envisioned this as THE BIG BOOK OF EVERYDAY RESISTANCE, so maybe that will come true one day), I will put together an appendix of resistance sites and lists. Please, please feel free to email me with your own list and/or throughs, lori@riverdaleavebooks.com.

Until we meet again!

Carry On
By Jill Nagle

Carry on, and don't always keep calm, let
The tears flow
The rage burn
The despair swell
Steward those feelings as the children of our country's long history, too deep and rooted
To be excised with a single election, or 47.

Carry on, and dance your holy body with the earth as only you can
Perceive the trees, rooted, unmoved, grooming the air for our lungs
The winged and four-legged creatures still cawing, hissing, and barking life's name
Hold them as yourself and your loved ones, hearts first.

Carry on and step in
Again and again, to this, our only moment, ever
To our vast freedoms that still remain
To minister to ourselves and those we touch
To create the colors, sounds, smells, tastes, and textures
Of joy, peace, and healing.

Carry on and reach out
To the hands, hearts and ears longing to receive you
That we may link across miles, forming a bridge to the next world where
Over time, we craft collective reckoning with the lies, malfunctions, and history
That brought us here
So that we may truly choose
Elsewhere.

Carry on,
Carry on.
Carry on!

The poem appeared in the anthology *Anger is a Gift*.

About the Editor

Lori Perkins has been a newspaper editor, a literary agent, a book editor, a professor and an author for four decades. She considers herself a "word-slinger" because words are the ammunition that we all have. She encourages you all to use your power and fight the good fight.

This book will be updated periodically, so if you would like to contribute an essay and/or an editorial cartoon, please contact Perkins at lori@ riverdaleavebooks.com.

We hope that you enjoyed *The Book of Everyday Resistance*. Please, let us know what you think by taking the time to leave a review on either Amazon or Goodreads. Reviews and recommendations are the life's blood of the independent author and publisher.

Keep up with all things Riverdale Avenue Books at the link here, where you can find free books, exclusive promo codes and latest news:

https://preview.mailerlite.io/preview/1098983/sites/136486432257607665/0kJ9TD

Other Riverdale Avenue Books You Might Like

1984 in the 21st Century
Edited by Lori Perkins

#MeToo:
Essays About How and Why This Happened , What It Means and
How to Make Sure It Never Happens Again
Edited by Lori Perkins

Everything You Always Wanted to Know About Watergate
(But Were Afraid to Ask)
By Brian O'Connor and Lori Perkins

The Binge Watcher's Guide to The Handmaid's Tale
By Jamie Schmidt

The Binge Watcher's Guide to The West Wing: Seasons One and Two
By Joshua Stein, Ph.D.

The Binge Watcher's Guide to The Twilight Zone
By Jacob Trussell

The Binge Watcher's Guide to Black Mirror
By Marc Polite